BBC ACTIVE

GCSE BITESIZE

H45 126 396 2

D0313199

RELIGIOUS STUDIES

John Mayled
Libby Ahluwalia

Published by BBC Active, an imprint of Educational Publishers LLP, part of the Pearson Education Group
Edinburgh Gate, Harlow, Essex CN20 2JE, England

ISBN: 978-1-4066-1376-6

Printed in China GCC/01

The Publisher's policy is to use paper manufactured from sustainable forests.

First published 2002
This edition 2007

Contents

About Bitesize

GCSE Bitesize is a revision service designed to help you achieve success at GCSE. There are books, television programmes and a website, each of which provides a separate resource designed to help you get the best results.

TV programmes are available on video through your school, or you can find out transmission times by calling **08700 100 222**.

The website can be found at
http://www.bbc.co.uk/schools/gcsebitesize/re

About this book

This book is your all-in-one revision companion for GCSE.
It gives you the three things you need for successful revision:

1 every topic, clearly organised and clearly explained
2 the most important facts and ideas highlighted for quick checking
3 all the practice you need – in the check questions in the margins, in the practice section at the end of each topic, and in the exam questions section at the end of this book.

Each topic is organised in the same way:

■ **The bare bones** – a summary of the main points, an introduction to the topic, and a good way to check what you know

■ **Key facts** highlighted throughout

■ **Check questions** in the margin at the end of each section of the topic - have you understood this bit?

■ **Remember tips** in the margin – extra advice on this section of the topic

■ **Exam tips** in red – specific things to bear in mind for the exam

■ **Practice questions** at the end of each topic – a range of questions to check your understanding.

The extra sections at the back of this book will help you check your progress and be confident that you know your stuff:

■ a selection of **Exam questions and model answers** explained to help you get full marks, plus extra questions for you to try for yourself, with answers

■ a **Topic checker** with quick questions in all topic areas

■ a **Complete the facts** section

■ a **Last-minute learner** – the most important facts in just four pages.

How to revise for GCSE Religious Studies

There are three main aspects to successful revision. You will waste less time and achieve better results if you bear in mind the following: **organise** – prepare a long-term plan in order to make the most of your time; **learn** – make sure you know the relevant facts; and **apply** – understand and practise how to answer different types of questions.

Organise

You need to draw up a revision timetable to cover all your subjects – not just Religious Studies! It should begin three or four months (not days!) before your exams start. Your school may produce one which you could use, or you could adapt one to suit your own needs. Once you've drawn up an outline timetable, divide the days (say, 90 or 100) by the number of subjects you are taking. This will tell you how many days you have for revising Religious Studies.

Three very important things about revision are:

1 **Do not revise for more than about forty minutes at a time without a break** as you will get too tired to learn properly. About three forty-minute sessions per night is enough for most people. Make sure you take breaks of at least ten or fifteen minutes between each session.

2 **Be realistic** – plan to have some time off, as well as time for revision. One complete day off and one night off a week is reasonable if you have started your revision early enough. Your work will be easier to remember if you come back to it from a break, and you need some time to relax with your friends. Don't forget to eat properly and get some fresh air and exercise every day!

3 **Try to stick to your plan.** If you cannot do the revision planned for a particular day because of illness or some other reason, re-organise your timetable to take account of this. If you start your revision early enough, there should be enough time to allow for unexpected illness, guests or other interruptions. However, be careful that you don't spend more time making new revision plans than you do on the revising itself!

Learn

Instead of copying out your notes or just reading your textbook, try some other ways of revising:

■ highlight or underline key terms and facts in your notes

■ write these key points on index cards, perhaps using brightly-coloured pens

■ read out the main points into a tape recorder, and then play it back

■ ask someone to test you on a topic

Learn *continued*

■ make colourful diagrams of the main points and key facts and put the diagrams up on the wall in your bedroom or somewhere else where they will catch your eye.

Try the following method to learn new vocabulary.

1 Make two sets of cards in different colours, for example, use one piece of A4 card in blue and another in red.

2 Cut the pieces of A4 into smaller cards.

3 Write the new words on the blue cards and their meanings on the red cards.

4 Shuffle the cards and then try to match each blue word card with its red partner.

You could do this with a friend and see who can make the most pairs in the shortest time. Or you could take turns to test each other, reading out the meanings on the red cards and getting the other person to give you the right word.

Whatever methods you use for revision, try to find a warm, quiet place away from distractions. You will probably find that using several techniques to revise a topic is more interesting than using the same method over and over again.

Apply

Practising written answers to exam-type questions is just as important as learning the facts. For a revision session, you could work through an example question. Make sure you look at and work through the variety of different kinds of questions, rather than concentrating on just one kind.

1 **Questions that test your knowledge of facts** – for these questions, you have to give information, perhaps about the beliefs of the religion you have been studying, or perhaps about the place of worship, the work of a charity, a festival or some other topic.

2 **Questions that test your understanding of how religious belief affects people's lives** – these questions ask you to show that you understand the effects of a religion on its members, for example, showing how beliefs affect behaviour or how a religious believer might feel about something.

3 **Questions that test your ability to evaluate** – these questions ask for your opinion and the opinions of religious believers. You need to practise giving your reasons as well as just saying what you think. Think about explaining how a religious believer might answer the question and show you understand their reasons. You might find it useful to get a friend to mark it for you, while you mark theirs. Talk about how your answers are different, and why you think one answer is better than the other.

Even if you have finished having lessons and are on study leave, you could write practice answers and take them into school to show to your teacher and ask for comments. Check first that your teacher will be available on the day and at the time that you plan to visit!

On the day

Make sure that you get to bed at a reasonable time the night before an exam and don't try to stay up too late to revise. Ask someone to check that you don't oversleep and remember to eat a proper breakfast. Take two or three blue or black pens with you (do not use other colours) and allow yourself plenty of time to get to the exam.

If your exam paper is divided into sections, make sure that you know which sections you have been prepared for. Make sure that you know how long the exam will last, how many questions you have to answer and whether any of them are compulsory. Divide your time carefully and make sure that you spend the most time on the questions that are worth the most marks.

Jot down a few notes (not too many) as a plan for each answer before you start to write. If you cannot think of anything to write in your notes, you have still got time to choose a different question! Read the questions carefully and make sure you understand what you are being asked to do.

If you are unsure of an answer, write something, even if it states the obvious, but never leave an answer blank – you cannot be given any marks for writing nothing. Remember – the examiners want to see how much you can do and are not trying to catch you out! They will try and give you marks wherever they can.

Good luck!

REMEMBER Throughout this book, where dates are referred to, the abbreviation BCE (Before Common Era) is used instead of BC (Before Christ), and CE (Common Era) instead of AD (Anno Domini).

This book covers only Christianity. This is because it is the most popular religion to be studied in schools. However, you may also be studying another religion. In this case, the revision tips in this section will be just as useful to you in revising for that religion.

Acknowledgements

Every effort has been made to trace the copyright holders of the material used in this book. If, however, any omissions have been made, we would be happy to rectify this. Please contact us at the address on the title page. We would like to thank the following:

John Stillwell/PA Photos, p. 23; Jon Arnold/Getty Images, p. 28; Robert Harding World Imagery/Alamy, p. 29; David Young-Wolff/Getty Images, p. 58; Rob Crandell/Alamy, p. 62; St Christopher's Hospice, p. 66; Nick Cobbing/Alamy, p. 74; Barry Batchelor/PA Photos, p. 83; Christian Aid, p. 52; Tearfund, p. 52; Cafod, p. 53; Amnesty International, p. 71.

God and the idea of the Trinity

➤ Christians are monotheists; they believe that there is only one God.

➤ Christians believe that, although there is only one God, He can be understood in three different ways: God the Father, God the Son, and God the Holy Spirit. These three together are called the Trinity.

A What is the Trinity?

When Christians talk about the Trinity they are referring to the way in which God is described and how people understand what God is.

Christians believe in one god who has three 'persons' or 'natures'.

> Father — is not — Son
> is / is
> is not / God / is not
> is / is not
> Holy Spirit

Although these are different, they are all part of the same God.

Many people have found the Trinity a very difficult idea to understand. The important point to remember is that although God is described as three persons, there is still only one God, not three different ones.

KEY FACT

Remember
The Trinity is the idea that there are three persons who are all God, not three Gods.

Q Who are the three 'persons' of the Trinity?

B Why do Christians believe in the idea of the Trinity?

Christians say that the idea of the Trinity is found in the Bible where God is described in three different ways.

All the Creeds of the Christian Church, such as the Apostles' Creed and the Nicene Creed, talk about the Trinity.

KEY FACT

The Trinity is a way of expressing the different personalities of God which are found in the Bible and in Christian teaching.

C What are the three persons of the Trinity?

God the Father is believed to be the **creator** of the universe. God is also called Father as **a way of showing human dependence on God**, denoting a close and loving relationship.

God the Son refers to **Jesus**. Christians believe that Jesus was not just an ordinary man, but was **God in human form**. Christians believe that the death and resurrection of Jesus made it possible for them to have salvation.

God the Holy Spirit refers to **the way in which God lives in the hearts and lives of believers.** Christians believe that God sent his Holy Spirit to comfort and guide people, so that when they pray, God answers them and gives them the courage to do the right thing.

Remember
Jesus was a human being, but he was also God.

Q Can you think of another way to show the Trinity as a diagram or picture?

EY FACT

D Alternative ideas about God

- Traditionally, people have referred to God as being a man and so we have the idea in Christianity of God the Father.

> In recent years, many women have objected to this saying that as everyone is made in God's image, God should be thought of as female as well as male.

- Therefore, some people now use the expression God the Mother in their prayers. They feel that this shows that God has a more feminine side.

1 What do Christians mean when they talk about the Trinity?

2 Where might you look to find teachings about the Trinity?

> Remember that the three persons of the Trinity are all God.

The Bible

THE BARE BONES

➤ The Bible is the most important and holy book in Christianity.

➤ Christians believe that the Bible is the 'Word of God', and a way in which God communicates to humanity.

➤ Christians try to understand the messages of the Bible, and to put them into practice in their daily lives.

A   What is the Bible?

KEY FACT

> The Christian scriptures, which are usually called the Old Testament and the New Testament, are called the Bible.

The **Old Testament** contains 39 books which together make up the whole of the Jewish Bible – the Tenakh. Jews refer to the first five books of their scriptures – Genesis, Exodus, Leviticus, Numbers and Deuteronomy – as the Torah (law).

They believe that these books were given to Moses by God.

The **New Testament** is the writings of some of the first Christians.

KEY FACT

> The New Testament contains Christian teachings about the life and death of Jesus, and what it means to be a Christian.

Q What is the Tenakh?

The 27 individual books of the New Testament were probably written in the first hundred years after the death of Jesus, but were not brought together until 367 CE.

B   What do Christians believe about the Bible?

Remember
Although Christians may have different ideas about whether the Bible is literally true, they all try to follow its teachings.

1 Some Christians believe that the Bible is literally true. This means that they think that everything in the Bible happened in exactly the way that it is described. They believe that if scientists or historians have different understandings of the world, it is the Bible which is right and the people who are wrong, because they think that people make mistakes but God never does.

• These Christians are often called 'fundamentalists' or 'creationists'. They might have difficulties when passages in the Bible seem to be contradicted by modern evidence.

2 Other Christians believe that parts of the Bible are not literally true, but are true in other ways, perhaps as stories that teach us crucial things about life. They believe that, sometimes, the Bible displays an understanding of the world that is outdated now.

KEY FACT

> For Christians, the Bible is the Word of God. It is a 'revealed' text which means that it was revealed by God to humans.

c The Old and the New Testament

Remember

Christians believe that the Bible is the Word of God. Some people believe every word of the Bible is the literal truth while others believe that is has to be interpreted because it can sometimes be out-of-date.

- **Jesus was a Jew**, as were his followers. For this reason, the Old Testament is very important.

- It contains history, law, poetry and prophecy.

- One of its major themes is the relationship between God and humanity. The prophets wrote about the coming of a Messiah, who would bring peace to the earth.

- Isaiah wrote about a Servant of God who would suffer for the people's sins. Christians believe that this servant was Jesus.

- The first four books are the Gospels of Matthew, Mark, Luke and John. Gospels means 'good news'. The gospels are about the main events in the life of Jesus.

- The next book is the Acts of the Apostles.

- There are 21 books which are called the Epistles, or letters.

- The final book of the New Testament is the Apocalypse or Book of Revelation and is a book of prophecy about what will happen during the last days of the world.

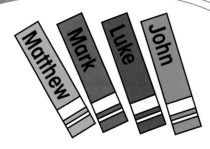

Many Christians read some of the Bible every day and they use it as a guide when making important decisions.

Q How do Christians use the Bible in their daily lives?

KEY FACT

1 Explain what is meant by the Old and New Testaments.

2 What do Christians believe about the Bible?

Remember the Bible is in two parts, the Old Testament and the New Testament and it is the New Testament which is about Jesus and his teachings.

Jesus

THE BARE BONES

➤ The life of Jesus is an essential part of the Christian faith and there are a number of key events which are very important.

➤ Christians believe that Jesus Christ was the Son of God.

A Who was Jesus?

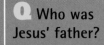
KEY FACT

Christians believe that Jesus was the Son of God. They believe that Jesus was God incarnate, which means God in human form.

They also believe that God came to the Earth as a man to live amongst other people, to teach them and to share in their sufferings.

Remember
Jesus' mother was Mary but his father was God.

- Jesus was born sometime between 8 and 6 BCE, in the town of Bethlehem in Judaea, Palestine.

- Jesus' mother was a young woman called Mary. His father was a carpenter called Joseph but although Joseph was responsible for bringing up the young boy, the Bible teaches that his real father was God.

- We know very little about Jesus until he was aged about thirty. He visited his cousin, John the Baptist, and was baptized by him. It was then that his work started and his followers began to believe that Jesus was the Son of God.

Q Who was Jesus' father?

B What did Jesus do?

- After his Baptism, Jesus went into the wilderness for forty days to prepare himself for his ministry. Here he was tempted by the devil who offered riches and power if Jesus would follow him rather than God.

...mber

- Jesus gathered around him a group of men who are known as the Twelve Disciples. They were all working men from Galilee.

Simon Peter, Andrew, John, Philip, James the son of Zebedee, Bartholomew, Thomas, Matthew, James the son of Alphaeus, Thaddaeus, Simon, Judas Iscariot.

Jesus preached in the open and attracted enormous crowds wherever he went. He performed many miracles during his ministry in Galilee, in particular healing the sick and the lame and making the blind see.

- Most of his teaching was in parables. These were stories which his listeners could easily understand, but which had a very important message. A good example is the famous story of the Good Samaritan (Luke 10: 29-37).

...year ...e die...

The Crucifixion of Jesus

- Jesus angered the Jewish authorities with his teaching and the Jewish priests were alarmed by the claim that Jesus was the Messiah. They expected the Messiah to be a king leading an army to free them from the rule of the Romans and Jesus was nothing at all like this.

- At the time of the feast of the Passover, Jesus celebrated a special meal with his disciples, the Last Supper. He was betrayed to the soldiers of the High Priest by Judas Iscariot. The High Priest and the elders (the Sanhedrin) tried Jesus and he was then taken before Pontius Pilate, the Roman Governor.

- Pilate was reluctant to execute Jesus but the Jewish priests were so insistent on his guilt that Pilate was finally forced to sentence him to death. Jesus was crucified on Good Friday.

- A rich follower of Jesus, Joseph of Arimathea, had Jesus' body taken away and placed in a private tomb. The Sabbath began that evening, so it was not until Sunday morning that anyone could visit the tomb.

- When three women arrived at the tomb on Sunday they found that the stone covering the entrance had been rolled away. At first they thought someone had stolen the body but, shortly afterwards, they met Jesus. He had risen from the dead.

- Jesus met with his disciples and other followers, and ate and talked with them for another 40 days. Then he was taken up into heaven and they did not see him on earth again.

- When Jesus' disciples gathered together to celebrate the festival of Pentecost they received the Holy Spirit. This appeared as tongues of flame over them and they found that they could speak in different languages so that they could spread the teachings of Jesus.

Jesus was a man, but he was also God.

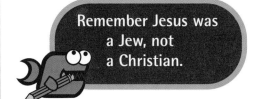
Remember Jesus was a Jew, not a Christian.

KEY FACT

1 What was special about the birth of Jesus?

2 What important teaching is found in the Parable of the Good Samaritan?

The Ten Commandments

THE BARE BONES

➤ The Ten Commandments are ten rules which Jews and Christians believe were made by God.

➤ They were given to Moses to pass on to everyone else.

A What are the Ten Commandments?

The Ten Commandments are found in several places in the Old Testament, including Exodus 20.

Remember
Jesus said he did not want to change the Ten Commandments in any way.

- You shall not commit adultery.
- You shall have no other gods.
- You shall not misuse the name of God.
- You shall not covet (be envious of) your neighbour's possessions.
- Honour your father and mother
- You shall not worship idols.
- You shall not murder.
- Remember the Sabbath day and keep it holy.
- You shall not give false testimony against your neighbour.
- You shall not steal.

B What do they mean?

- Four of the commandments are about **how people should behave towards God:**

    You shall have no other gods.

    You shall not worship idols.

    You shall not misuse the name of God.

    Remember the Sabbath day and keep it holy.

- The other six are about **how people should treat each other:**

    Honour your father and mother.

    You shall not murder.

    You shall not commit adultery.

    You shall not steal.

    You shall not give false testimony against your neighbour.

    You shall not covet (be envious of) your neighbour's possessions.

- For both Jews and Christians, **all of the commandments are equally important.**

Q Which of the commandments do you feel is the most important and why?

C Why are the Ten Commandments important?

The Ten Commandments are part of the 'covenant', or agreement, made between God and humanity.

KEY FACT

Remember
The Ten Commandments are just as important for Christians today as they were for the Israelites in the desert.

KEY FACT

Q Who did God give the Ten Commandments to?

KEY FACT

- The Ten Commandments were given by God to Moses as a set of rules for life. They apply to everyone, all of the time.

- If people obeyed these rules, God would be pleased with them and take care of them.

- If people disobeyed the rules then God would punish them. There are several examples in the Old Testament of people being punished for breaking some of the commandments.

Many of our laws today are still based on the Ten Commandments.

- In synagogues and also in many churches the Ten Commandments are written on the walls so that people are always reminded that these were the Laws which God gave to humanity and which all people must keep in order to obey God.

Jews and Christians believe that these rules apply to everyone all the time, and give an outline of the right way to live.

1 Why do you think God gave his people the Ten Commandments?

2 Explain why the fourth commandment is important.

Jesus said that the two greatest commandments were 'to love God and to love your neighbour as yourself'. Although these are not part of the original Ten Commandments, they do, in fact, summarise them.

THE BARE BONES

➤ Jesus delivered a sermon usually called the Sermon on the Mount when he was near to the Sea of Galilee (Matthew 5–7).

➤ During this sermon he taught people the Beatitudes and the Lord's Prayer.

Beatitudes:

Blessed are the poor in spirit, for their's is the kingdom of heaven.

Blessed are those who mourn, for they will be comforted.

Blessed are the meek, for they will inherit the earth.

Blessed are those who hunger and thirst for righteousness, for they will be filled.

Blessed are the merciful, for they will be shown mercy.

Blessed are the pure in heart, for they will see God.

Blessed are the peacemakers, for they will be called sons of God.

Blessed are those who are persecuted because of righteousness, for theirs is the kingdom of heaven.

Blessed are you when people insult you, persecute you and falsely say all kinds of evil against you because of me. Rejoice and be glad, because great is your reward in heaven, for in the same way, they persecuted the prophets who were before you. (Matthew 5:3–12)

Jesus explained that although people often had to suffer in their lives on earth, God loved them and they would be rewarded and comforted when they died and went to heaven.

B What is the Lord's Prayer?

Jesus said people often made a great fuss about praying, and prayed in public so other people would see them and see how holy they were. He said that this was wrong and told people that they should pray using the Lord's Prayer.

...h ...eded.

...Where did ...sus preach the ...ermon on the Mount?

'Our Father in heaven,
hallowed be your name,
your kingdom come,
your will be done
on earth as it is in heaven.
Give us today our daily bread.

Forgive us our debts,
as we also have forgiven our debtors.
And lead us not into temptation,
but deliver us from the evil one.'
(Matthew 6:9–13)

c *What other teachings are in the Sermon on the Mount?*

1 Jesus taught people not to judge others.

'Do not judge, or you too will be judged. For in the same way as you judge others, you will be judged, and with the measure you use, it will be measured to you.' (Matthew 7:1–2)

2 He taught that adultery and divorce were wrong.

'It has been said, "Anyone who divorces his wife must give a certificate of divorce". But I tell you that anyone who divorces his wife, except for marital unfaithfulness, causes her to become an adultress, and anyone who marries the divorced woman commits adultery'. (Matthew 5:43–45)

3 He also taught that people should forgive others.

'You have heard that it was said, "Love your neighbour and hate your enemy". But I tell you: Love your enemies and pray for those who persecute you, that you may be sons of your Father in heaven.' (Matthew 5:43–45)

The Sermon on the Mount contains almost all of the important teachings which Jesus gave to his followers.

1 Why did Jesus say people should use the Lord's Prayer?

2 What did Jesus teach about divorce?

When you answer a question on the Sermon on the Mount, remember there are many other things in the sermon apart from the Beatitudes.

The problem of evil

THE BARE BONES

> The problem of evil asks how people can believe in a loving, all-powerful God when there is evil and suffering in the world.

> Did God create evil? Does God make us suffer on purpose? Or, is there nothing God can do to prevent it?

A   Moral evil and natural evil

KEY FACT

Philosophers often draw a distinction between moral evil and natural evil.

- **Moral evil** is the name given to evil which is deliberately caused by humans, such as cruelty or dishonesty.

- **Natural evil** is the name given to bad things which happen but which are not anyone's deliberate fault, such as earthquakes and floods and diseases.

KEY FACT

Many people think that the existence of evil and suffering in the world shows that there is no God, or, if there is a God, he isn't very kind. Christians have to try and find a way of answering them.

Where was God during the Holocaust, or the war in Bosnia, or when the World Trade Centre was hit?

Why do animals or babies suffer, when they can't be expected to learn anything from it?

If God can do miracles, why doesn't he do them all the time, whenever people are suffering?

'The problem of evil'

Does God need to test people, before he knows how strong their faith is? Shouldn't God know that already?

Q Explain the difference between 'natural' and 'moral' evil

If God knows that some people are going to suffer a lot, or be very evil people, why does he make them in the first place?

Why do some people suffer so much more than others?

B   Why does God allow suffering?

Remember
Many Christians say that evil can't be understood – we just have to trust God knows what he's doing.

- Sometimes Christians say the world was made perfect, but that people disobeyed God. This disobedience is known as **the Fall**. They sometimes argue the Fall was such a catastrophe that it spoilt the balance of nature as well as the relationship between people and God – so people are responsible for natural disasters as well as for the wrong choices they make. This way of thinking follows the Christian teacher **Augustine**.

B

- Another Christian approach to the problem of evil is to say that God deliberately gave people **free will**. If people were going to have a real freedom to choose, then there had to be the possibility of doing wrong, otherwise the choice would only be pretend.

- Sometimes people say that if there was no evil and suffering in the world, then we would not **develop** as human beings. We couldn't be brave unless there was danger. We couldn't be generous if there were no people who needed things. We would never learn important lessons such as how to be patient, if we always got what we wanted. This way of thinking follows the Christian teacher **Irenaeus**.

- Some people say that suffering is **a kind of test** from God, to see how people will respond and if they will stay faithful. But others disagree with this idea, saying that God already knows everything and doesn't need to test us in this way.

- Some Christians believe that evil in the world is the fault of **the Devil**. They believe that the Devil encourages people to do wrong, and that the Devil causes disease and natural disasters. Other Christians believe that the Devil is a way of describing the opposite of God, but they do not think that the Devil literally exists as a personality, because this would suggest that God doesn't have the power to do anything to stop him.

Q Why do some Christians find it difficult to believe in the idea of a personal Devil?

C *Suffering in the Bible: the Book of Job*

The Bible presents different approaches to evil and suffering. One of the most famous is the story of Job. Job was a good man who was faithful to God, but God allowed Satan (the Devil) to test Job by making him suffer. Job lost all his wealth, his family and his home, but still he remained faithful to God. However, he wanted to know why God was allowing him to suffer, and he demanded to meet God and to ask him. God told him that as creator of the world, he was so much more powerful than Job, and Job should recognise that he had no right to challenge God. Job understood that he should just accept his suffering, and everything was restored to him.

Q What is the main message of the story of Job?

KEY FACT

Many stories in the Bible show that God does not like to see people suffer.

- Christians believe God answers prayers when people ask for help. Jesus healed people who were sick, and brought dead people back to life.

1 Explain how Christians have tried to answer the problem of why a loving God allows evil in the world.

2 Explain Biblical teaching about evil and suffering.

3 'All the evil in the world must come from the Devil.' Do you agree? Give reasons to support your answer, and show you have thought about different points of view. You must refer to Christianity in your answer.

The Church - history

THE BARE BONES

➤ The Christian church has developed over nearly 2000 years since the death of Jesus.

➤ There are many different divisions and groups in the Church.

A Early history

Remember

Jesus was a Jew who may not have intended to found a new religion. His early followers were Jews and it was after Paul's conversion that the message of Christianity was preached to both Jews and gentiles (non-Jews).

Q When did the Orthodox and Roman Catholic churches split?

Remember

Originally Christianity was based in Byzantium, Roman capital, Rome.

3BCE — Jesus of Nazareth – Jesus Christ – was probably born around the year 3 BCE in Bethlehem in the Roman province of Judaea in what is now Israel.

He was **crucified** around 30 CE by the Romans. — 30CE

— 35CE

One day while on the road to Damascus, probably in **35 CE**, Saul had a vision that Jesus called him. His name was changed to **Paul** and he began to preach the message of Christianity throughout the **Mediterranean**.

In **250 CE**, people began to bring together the 27 books of the **New Testament**. — 250CE

A Jew, **Saul of Tarsus**, was employed to hunt out and persecute these early followers of Jesus.

In **300 CE**, persecution of **Christians** began in the Roman Empire. — 300CE
— 392CE

In **392 CE**, the Roman Emperor Theodosius I made Christianity the **official religion** of the Roman Empire.

In **597 CE**, Augustine came to **England** and brought Christianity to the country.

— 597CE

In 1054 CE there was a **split** between the churches in Rome and Byzantium over differences in teaching. These two groups became the **Roman Catholic Church** based in **Rome** with the **Pope** as its head and the **Orthodox Church** based in **Byzantium** under the **Patriarch of Constantinople**. — 1054CE

By the **14th** and **15th centuries**, some theologians in Europe began to question the power of the Pope and some of the doctrines of the church. In particular, the practice of the 'selling of indulgences' (see Key terms) was criticised.

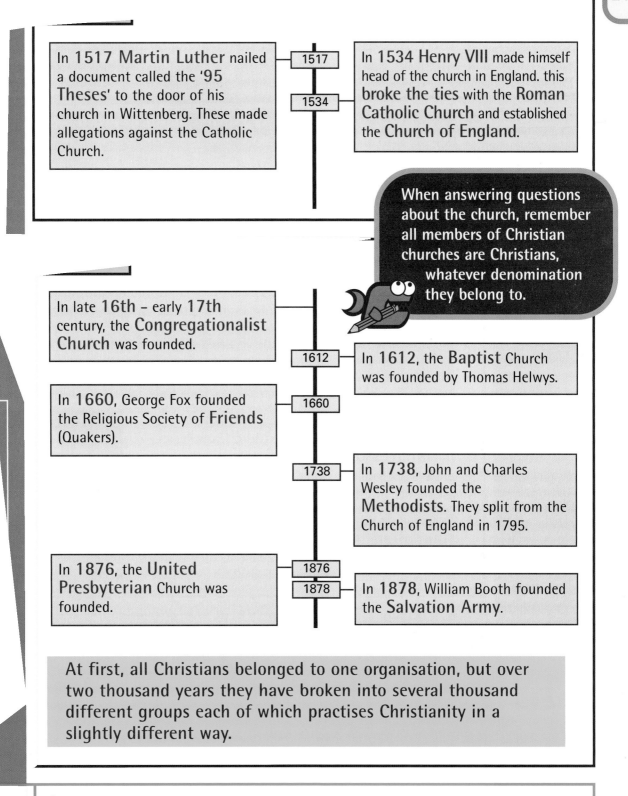

In 1517 Martin Luther nailed a document called the '95 Theses' to the door of his church in Wittenberg. These made allegations against the Catholic Church.

1517

1534

In 1534 Henry VIII made himself head of the church in England. this broke the ties with the Roman Catholic Church and established the Church of England.

When answering questions about the church, remember all members of Christian churches are Christians, whatever denomination they belong to.

In late 16th – early 17th century, the Congregationalist Church was founded.

1612

In 1612, the Baptist Church was founded by Thomas Helwys.

In 1660, George Fox founded the Religious Society of Friends (Quakers).

1660

1738

In 1738, John and Charles Wesley founded the Methodists. They split from the Church of England in 1795.

In 1876, the United Presbyterian Church was founded.

1876

1878

In 1878, William Booth founded the Salvation Army.

At first, all Christians belonged to one organisation, but over two thousand years they have broken into several thousand different groups each of which practises Christianity in a slightly different way.

1 Who was Saul and what happened to him?
2 Give two reasons that Christians have split into different groups.

Christian denominations

THE BARE BONES
- There are several thousand different denominations in Christianity.
- All these people are Christians who believe in the Trinity and that Jesus was the Son of God.
- The difference between these denominations is found in some of their beliefs and practices.

A Roman Catholic church

KEY FACTS

The Roman Catholic church is based in Rome and has the Pope as its head.

It is believed that the Pope is in a direct line from St Peter who founded the church in Rome and, therefore, he has the authority of the apostles of Jesus.

The Pope is the spiritual leader of the Roman Catholic Church and is responsible for all the rulings and teachings which it issues.

- As well as their belief in the spiritual authority of the Pope, the Roman Catholic church believes in the **intercessory power of the saints** and so prayers are said, for example, to the Virgin Mary, asking her to intercede with Jesus.

- The Roman Catholic church also teaches **transubstantiation**. This means that when the bread and wine are consecrated at the eucharist, they actually become the body and blood of Jesus.

B Protestant churches

KEY FACTS

The Protestant denomination includes many churches such as the Anglican church (Church of England), Baptists, Methodists and United Reformed Church.

- In 1517, **Martin Luther** was responsible for the beginning of the **Reformation**. He believed much of the Roman Catholic church was corrupt and was not following God's teachings.

The Reformation, which saw the division between the Roman Catholic and Protestant churches, was a split away from Rome.

Q Who is the head of the Roman Catholic Church?

- The Protestant churches do not recognise the authority of the Pope and instead have their own religious leaders.

C Church of England

- The Church of England came into existence in 1534 when **King Henry VIII**, made himself head of the church.
He had an argument with the Pope because he wanted a divorce which the Roman Catholic church would not allow. This broke the ties with the Roman Catholic Church and established the Church of England.

Remember
Christians believe in the Trinity and that Jesus was the Son of God.

EY FACT

The spiritual head of the Church of England is the Archbishop of Canterbury, while the temporal head of the Church is the ruling monarch of Great Britain.

D Non-conformist churches

Q Why do you think there are so many different groups or denominations of Christians?

- There are many different non-conformist denominations. These include the Baptists, Methodists, United Reformed Church and the Quakers. Non-conformists are churches which do not 'conform' or belong to one of the main churches such as the Roman Catholic, Orthodox or Anglican churches.

- Most of these groups do not recognise an overall spiritual leader and some of their communities are completely independent of any organisation.

EY FACT

All of these groups came into existence because a particular preacher or group of Christians wanted to come together and worship in a particular way.

1 Why did the Protestant churches split from the Roman Catholic church.

2 Why did the Church of England come into existence?

When you answer questions about Christian denominations, remember to treat all denominations as being equal. They all follow the teachings of Jesus.

Ecumenism

THE BARE BONES

> Ecumenism is the name given to the belief that all churches should try to become more united. It is a movement which encourages Christians to worship together and forget their differences.

A What issues do Christians disagree about?

1 The authority of the Pope – some Christians believe that the Pope is the head of the Church and that Christians should accept his authority. Others disagree.

2 The ordination of women – some Christians believe that women should have an equal role with men in Christian ministry. Others believe that men and women have different talents, and that women should not be allowed to celebrate the Eucharist (Holy Communion).

3 The Eucharist – some Christians believe that when the bread and wine are blessed by the priest, they become the actual body and blood of Jesus. Other Christians believe that they are symbols used to remember Jesus' sacrifice on the cross.

> There are many issues which divide Christians and cause disagreements.

Remember
It is issues such as the eucharist, the ordination of women and the authority of the Pope which divide Christains.

KEY FACT

B What is the World Council of Churches?

- The World Council of Churches was formed after the Second World War, in 1948, by Christians who wanted to do something about restoring peace in the world. The people wanted to **promote ecumenism** by encouraging Christians to work more closely together.

- Many Christians believe it is important to work together, because disagreements and divisions give a bad impression of Christianity's message of love, and prevent Christians from doing important things such as caring for the poor.

- The World Council of Churches was set up to promote unity, to act as a Christian voice in the world, and to help bring about peace and justice in accordance with Christian principles.

Remember
The World Council of Churches was set up in 1948 to help bring peace after the Second World War.

- All the main Christian Churches, apart from the Roman Catholic Church, belong to the World Council of Churches. They aim to listen to each other and to learn from each other, in the hope that they will grow together rather than apart. They try to emphasise their shared beliefs as Christians, rather than their different ways of worship and different understandings of aspects of Christian teaching.

- The WCC holds meetings where members of all different denominations send representatives. They discuss all kinds of issues, such as refugees, the arms race, ecumenism, medical ethics and world debt.

- **Christian Aid** is the overseas aid agency for the World Council of Churches.

> **Ecumenism is the belief that although there are issues which divide Christians, they all share the same belief in Jesus and so should try to unite and work together.**

c Other ecumenical groups

- In 1972, the **United Reformed Church** was formed when the Congregationalists and the Presbyterians decided that they should join together and become one church rather than different denominations. Many Christians hoped that this would be the beginning of more unity amongst Christians.

- Some ecumenical centres have been established where Christians of all different denominations can worship together, no matter what sort of church they come from.

The Taizé community in France provides ecumenical worship for thousands of visitors every year. Services are conducted in several languages, and hymns and chants are sung together.

In the UK, the abbey on **the island of Iona** is used for youth camps and ecumenical worship.

- Both of these communities devote much of their time and income to helping the poor in developing countries.

1 Why do some Christians disagree with each other about the ordination of women?

2 What is an ecumenical centre?

> Remember in your answer that although Christians may belong to different churches they all have the same belief in Jesus and belong to the same religion.

The church – buildings and features

THE BARE BONES

➤ There are many different types of buildings in which Christians worship, often reflecting the style of worship which takes place inside them.

➤ Some buildings are very large and elaborate whilst others may be small and plain.

A Anglican and Roman Catholic churches

KEY FACT

These are often built in the shape of a cross, one of the main Christian symbols.

- The head of the cross is usually facing **east**, towards Jerusalem.
- The central part of the cross shape is know as the **nave**.
- Many churches have **spires** or **towers**. These are often seen as a sign of reaching up to God.
- All churches have a **font** where babies are brought to be baptised.

KEY FACT

The most important part of all Anglican and Roman Catholic churches is the altar, which is the holy table where the Eucharist is celebrated.

- Many Orthodox churches have onion domes on their roofs instead of spires or towers.

B Non-conformist churches

Remember
A Baptist church has a pool for baptisms instead of a font.

Q Explain how Meeting Houses differ from most other places of Christian worship.

- The buildings of the non-conformist denominations such as those of the Baptist, Methodist and United Reformed churches are often much plainer than Anglican or Roman Catholic buildings. They are usually called either **churches** or **chapels**.
- These churches will have a table for celebrating the Eucharist but the most important feature is the **pulpit**. It is from here that the Bible is read and sermons are preached. This stresses the importance of the **Ministry of the Word**.
- Most non-conformist buildings have a font, but in the **Baptist** church there is a large **pool** at the front of the building where adults are baptised by total immersion.
- The Quakers (Religious Society of Friends) meet to worship in a **Meeting House**. Quakers have a very simple style of worship where people sit in **silence** until one of them feels that the Holy Spirit wants them to speak.

KEY FACT

The buildings in which Christians worship are all designed to be 'the House of God' where Christians can come together and hear the words of God and pray.

c Interior features

- A Quaker Meeting House has a very plain interior and will usually only have **chairs** and a **table**.

- Anglican churches are often more elaborate. At the east end of the church, or sometimes in the very centre of the building, is the **altar** where the eucharist is celebrated. The **pulpit** for sermons and the **lectern** for the Bible may be either side of this. The **font** is usually placed at the west end of the church by the door.

- The most elaborate churches are usually Roman Catholic. In a Roman Catholic church, there are often several altars, **confessional boxes**, **statues** and many **candles**. There are **stained glass windows** illustrating stories from the Bible or the lives of the saints. On the walls are fourteen paintings or carvings representing the **Stations of the Cross** – important events in the last hours leading up to Jesus' crucifixion.

- Orthodox churches are similar in many ways to Roman Catholic churches except that there is an **iconostasis** or **screen** which separates the main part of the church from the altar. The iconostasis is decorated with **icons** (paintings) of Jesus and the saints and in the centre are the **Royal Doors** which are opened and closed during the services.

> When you are writing about a church building, remember to say which denomination it belongs to and why the different features are important to the members.

Remember
The most important part of a Roman Catholic or Anglican church is the altar where the Eucharist is celebrated.

Q Do you think churches should be elaborately decorated? Give reasons for your opinion.

---

1 What is the most important part of Roman Catholic and Anglican churches?

2 What is a font? What do some churches have instead of a font?

3 Why are many churches built in the shape of a cross?

4 Why do many churches have spires or towers?

Pilgrimage

➤ A pilgrimage is a religious journey. Usually people travel to places they believe have a special holy significance.

➤ Other Christians believe that a pilgrimage is a journey within.

A Why do Christians go on pilgrimage?

A pilgrimage is a religious journey. Some Christians go to special places while others say that their whole life is a pilgrimage towards God.

- Unlike some other religions, Christians are not expected or required to go on pilgrimage. It is a matter of **personal choice**.

- Pilgrimages are not holidays. Giving up time to go on pilgrimage might help to **strengthen a Christian's faith** and help them to lead better lives.

- Some Christians set aside time to make the journey because they feel this will help them **get closer to God** in a way that is not possible in their daily lives.

- Others go to special places where they hope they will **receive a cure** for an illness or disease or to pray for a cure for someone who is not well enough to travel.

B Where do Christians go on pilgrimage?

- In the Middle Ages, pilgrimage was very popular and many people travelled to cathedrals such as **St Albans** and **Canterbury**, to visit relics of the saints.

- Some people also travelled all the way to the **Holy Land** to see the places where Jesus lived, taught and died. Today many people still travel to the Holy Land to visit Bethlehem, Nazareth and Jerusalem. In Bethlehem, for instance, many Christians visit the Church of the Nativity which stands on the traditional site of the stable where Jesus was said to have been born.

B

• Another very important place of pilgrimage, especially for Roman Catholics, is **Lourdes** in France. A young girl called Bernadette Soubirous had a vision of the Virgin Mary here. A spring of water appeared where the vision had taken place and many people said they had been miraculously cured of illnesses after visiting this place. Many thousands of people go to Lourdes every year and pray for a miracle to heal themselves or others.

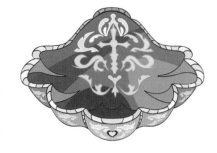

Remember
Some people make a pilgrimage in the hope of being cured of something or other people might go on their behalf if they are not well enough to travel.

• **Santiago de Compostela** in Spain became an important place of pilgrimage in the 9th century. Bones were found there which were believed to be from the body of the apostle James, John the Evangelist's brother. The bones were buried in a tomb under the high altar of the cathedral. 'Santiago' means St James and 'Compostela', field of stars. Pilgrims who visited Compostela wore a badge of a scallop shell which is the symbol of St James.

In your answer, remember that there are different reasons for Christians making a pilgrimage. You should explain what these are.

Q Who was St James?

1 Give some of the reasons why Christians might go on pilgrimage.

2 What do you think people mean when they say that a pilgrimage is a journey within?

Prayer

THE BARE BONES
➤ Prayer is communicating with God.
➤ Prayer is a very important aspect of life and worship for all Christians.

A What is prayer?

KEY FACT

> Prayer is communicating with God. This may be asking God for something or thanking God.

- Prayer is usually made in words, but not always, and can be public or private.

- Sometimes people pray together; this is known as corporate prayer. Sometimes people may pray quietly or silently when they are on their own.

B What types of prayer do Christians use?

- **Petitionary** prayer is when people ask God for something, for themselves or for other people.

- **Intercessory** prayer is when people ask God to intervene in the world at a time of crisis or when people are starving or suffering because of a disaster.

- Many prayers are said **to thank God** for creation and for life and existence in general. Other prayers are to ask God's help in leading a better life.

- Sometimes people use **formal set prayers** such as those found in the prayer books of the various churches.

- Many Christians pray **spontaneously**, taking an opportunity to speak to God.

Remember
There are several different types of prayer: intercessory, petitionary and prayers of thanksgiving.

> When answering questions about prayer, remember that prayers are not just to ask for something, many prayers are said to thank God for creation, for life and for sending his son, Jesus, to earth to save people from sin.

Q What is corporate prayer?

C Prayers

- The **Lord's Prayer**, which Jesus taught at the Sermon on the Mount, is one of the most important and well-known of Christian prayers. You can see the text of the prayer on page 16.

- The **'Jesus Prayer'** is often used in the Orthodox tradition:

> *Lord Jesus, Son of God*
> *be merciful to me, a sinner.*

- The **Hail Mary** is very popular with Roman Catholics:

> *Hail Mary, full of grace,*
> *the Lord is with thee.*
> *Blessed art thou among women*
> *and blessed is the fruit of they*
> *womb, Jesus.*
> *Holy Mary, Mother of God,*
> *pray for us sinners, now,*
> *and at the hour of our death.*
> *Amen.*

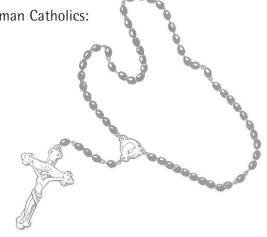

Remember
Jesus taught his disciples that when they prayed they should always say the Lord's prayer.

Praying is a way in which Christians feel they can **communicate with God**. As well as thanking God and asking for help, prayer makes people feel stronger because they believe they are having **a relationship and conversation with God** who will listen to them.

Q Why is prayer so important to Christians?

D ACTS

ACTS is one of the books in the New Testament. Some Christians pray in four parts which they remember as ACTS:

A: adoration – worshipping God

C: contrition – acknowledging what they may have done wrong

T: thanksgiving – thanking God

S: supplication – asking God for help.

1 List four different types of prayer.

2 Why do you think that the 'Hail Mary' is a popular prayer for some Christians?

Baptism

THE BARE BONES

➤ Baptism is the first of the seven sacraments (or religious rites) practised by many Christians.

➤ When a person is baptised, he or she is either sprinkled with, or totally immersed in, water as a sign of purification.

A What is a sacrament?

> A sacrament is a religious ceremony or act regarded as an outward and visible sign of inward and spiritual grace.

- The seven sacraments are:

baptism

confirmation

extreme unction (or last rites)

The Seven Sacraments

Eucharist (or communion)

matrimony

ordination

penance (or reconciliation)

- Before the Reformation, the seven sacraments were observed by all Christians. Today, Protestant churches tend to practise only baptism, the Eucharist and matrimony. However, Orthodox and Catholic churches still perform all seven sacraments.

> Most Christians believe that baptism is a sacrament, meaning an oath or sacred promise to God.

B Why do people need to be baptised?

> Christians believe that because of the disobedience of Adam and Eve in the garden of Eden all people are born with Original Sin and this needs to be removed before they can begin their lives as Christians.

Here is a part of the service recited during a Baptism ceremony.

> Our Lord Jesus Christ has told us
> that to enter the kingdom of heaven
> we must be born again of water and the Spirit,
> and has given us baptism as the sign and seal of this new birth.
> Here we are washed by the Holy Spirit and made clean.
> Here we are clothed with Christ,
> dying to sin that we may live his risen life.
> As children of God, we have a new dignity
> and God calls us to fullness of life. (*Common Worship*)

C   What happens at the baptism of a baby?

In most churches, cleansing of sin takes place when a young baby is baptised.

1 The baby is taken to church by its parents.

2 The priest and the family go to the font which is usually by the main door of the church.

3 As the baby cannot speak for itself, godparents make a promise that they will bring up the child as a Christian.

4 Next, the priest or minister blesses the baby and pours water over its head in the form of a cross, blessing it in the name of 'The Father, the Son and the Holy Spirit'.

D   What happens at the baptism of an adult?

1 Some Christians believe baptism should only take place when a person is able to make the decision for themselves. This is particularly true in the Baptist Church.

2 In the Baptist church, there is a ceremony of adult baptism. In the front of the church is a large tank or pool, covered by flooring. The pool is opened and the minister and the person to be baptised stand in it. The person is then baptised by total immersion. The minister holds them and they lean back right under the water.

This is the sort of baptism Jesus is supposed to have received from John the Baptist.

1 Why do babies need to be cleansed from sin?

2 What is different about baptism in a Baptist church?

The most important part of a baptism occurs when water is placed on the person's head and the priest says they are baptised in the name of 'The Father, the Son and the Holy Spirit'.

The Eucharist

THE BARE BONES

➤ The Eucharist is an important sacrament for many Christians.

➤ Christians have many different names for the Eucharist. These include: the Lord's Supper, Mass, Holy Communion and the Breaking of Bread.

A What is the Eucharist?

- The word 'Eucharist' comes from the Greek meaning 'thanksgiving'. It remembers Jesus' last meal with his disciples before he was crucified.

KEY FACT

> For many Christians, sharing in the Eucharist is the most important part of their worship together because it means they are united as they share the body and blood of Christ.

- In some churches the Eucharist is shared every day, but in others it happens once a week, once a month, or even more rarely.

B How is the Eucharist celebrated?

The celebration of the Eucharist usually follows a pattern:

- The bread and wine are placed on the altar and the priest or vicar reminds the congregation of what happened at the Last Supper.
- The Eucharistic Prayer is said, giving thanks to God.
- The bread and wine are blessed by the priest and the words of Jesus at the Last Supper are read.
- In some churches, the congregation exchange a sign of peace.
- The bread and wine are shared with the congregation.
- The congregation are blessed and 'sent out into the world'.

Remember
The Eucharist service recalls what happened during the Last Supper Jesus ate with his disciples.

Q What does 'Eucharist' mean?

C The Eucharistic Prayer

- Jesus words at the last supper.

> The Lord Jesus, on the night he was betrayed, took bread, and when he had given thanks, he broke it and said, 'This is my body, which is for you; do this in remembrance of me.' In the same way, after supper he took the cup, saying, 'This cup is the new covenant in my blood; do this, whenever you drink it, in remembrance of me.' (1 Corinthians 11:23–25)

KEY FACT

> Some Christians believe the bread and wine become the body and blood of Jesus when they are blessed. Others believe they symbolise Jesus' body and blood, but are bread and wine all the time.

- Here's one form of the Eucharistic Prayer:

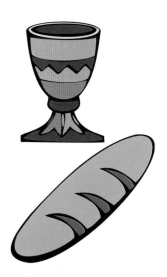

> Priest/Minister: The Lord be with you.
> **Congregation: And also with you.**
>
> Priest/Minister: Lift up your hearts.
> **Congregation: We lift them to the Lord.**
>
> Priest/Minister: Let us give thanks to the Lord our God.
> **Congregation: It is right to give thanks and praise.**
>
> Priest/Minister: It is indeed right,
> it is our duty and our joy,
> at all times and in all places
> to give you thanks and praise,
> holy Father, heavenly King,
> almighty and eternal God,
> through Jesus Christ your Son our Lord.

Q What do the bread and wine become?

---

1 What did Jesus say at the Last Supper when he broke bread and drank wine with his followers?

2 Give three alternative names for the Eucharist.

3 Why is the Eucharist such an important part of Christian worship?

Confirmation

THE BARE BONES
➤ Confirmation is one of the sacraments of the Christian Church.
➤ Confirmation celebrates the time when people decide for themselves to follow the Christian faith.

A What is confirmation?

- If people were baptised as Christians when they were babies, then confirmation gives them the opportunity to confirm for themselves, as adults, that the Christian religion is the one they want to follow.

KEY FACT

> Confirmation candidates make for themselves the promises that their parents and godparents made for them at baptism.

- Not all Christian denominations have confirmation ceremonies, because not all denominations have infant baptism. The churches which baptise adults do not feel there is a need for an extra ceremony to confirm promises already made at baptism.

Q Why might some people choose to be confirmed?

- Most people who are being confirmed prepare for this by going to **confirmation classes**. In these classes, they meet other people who are about to be confirmed, they learn about **what it means to be a Christian** and are taught about the promises they will make, so that they understand what it is they are promising.

B What happens at a confirmation?

KEY FACT

> A confirmation service is usually conducted by the Bishop.

1 The Bishop asks the confirmation candidates questions and they respond together:

Do you reject the devil and all rebellion against God?
I reject them.

Do you renounce the deceit and corruption of evil?
I renounce them.

Do you repent of the sins that separate us from God and neighbour?
I repent of them.

Do you turn to Christ as Saviour?
I turn to Christ.

Do you submit to Christ as Lord?
I submit to Christ.

Do you come to Christ, the way, the truth and the life?
I come to Christ.

Remember
A sacrament
an outward
visible sig
inward s
grace.

2 The Bishop places his hands on the head of each person being confirmed, as a blessing. In some churches, he also puts some oil on their foreheads, as a sign of the Holy Spirit.

3 The bishop extends his hands towards those to be confirmed and says:

> Almighty and ever-living God,
> you have given these your servants new birth
> in baptism by water and the Spirit,
> and have forgiven them all their sins.
> Let your Holy Spirit rest upon them:
> the Spirit of wisdom and understanding;
> the Spirit of counsel and inward strength;
> the Spirit of knowledge and true godliness;
> and let their delight be in the fear of the Lord. Amen.

4 The bishop addresses each candidate by name.

> [Name], God has called you by name and made you his own.

5 He then lays his hand on the head of each, saying:

> Confirm, O Lord, your servant with your Holy Spirit. Amen.

6 The bishop invites the congregation to pray for all those on whom hands have been laid.

> Defend, O Lord, these your servants with your heavenly grace,
> that they may continue yours for ever,
> and daily increase in your Holy Spirit more and more
> until they come to your everlasting kingdom. Amen.

1 Why do people go to confirmation classes before being confirmed?

2 Why do some Christian denominations not have confirmation?

3 Explain what happens at a confirmation service.

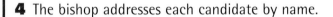

In the exam, you should explain why some denominations do not have confirmation.

THE BARE BONES

➤ Christians believe that death is not the end of a person, although it is the end of their life on earth.

➤ The Bible teaches it is through faith in Jesus and his sacrifice that Christians have the chance of going to heaven.

A What is a funeral for?

Christian funerals reflect the belief that death is not the end of a person. Although people are sad because a friend, relative or colleague has died, they are encouraged to think about the promise of resurrection and eternal life made by Jesus. They ask for God's comfort, and thank him for the good qualities the person had, rather than concentrating only on sadness.

KEY FACT

Although a funeral service shows respect for the body of the dead person, it really marks the time when a Christian's soul moves from earth to heaven.

B What happens at a funeral?

- A Christian funeral is usually held a few days after a person has died. This is to allow time for people to be contacted and make arrangements to attend.

- Christianity does not have rules about whether people should be buried or cremated, this is a matter of individual preference.

- A Christian funeral service begins with the vicar or priest reminding the congregation of the words of Jesus: 'I am the resurrection and the life'. This stresses the fact that it is through faith in Jesus and his sacrifice on the cross that Christians have the chance of going to heaven when they die.

- There are always prayers thanking God for the life of the person who has died, and asking God to comfort the people who remain.

- There are often hymns, and someone may give a short talk remembering the person who has died and the particular qualities he or she had.

- In Roman Catholic churches a special mass (Eucharist) is celebrated at the funeral service.

ember

R... ...ass is ce... ...ed to tha... God for the life of the person who has

Q What do Christians believe about death?

B

- In Western societies, friends and relatives often wear dark clothes as a symbol of sadness, but this is a custom rather than a religious rule. Some people prefer to have an atmosphere of celebration for life, and wear ordinary clothes rather than special black ones. It is also a custom to send flowers or wreaths to a funeral as a way of paying respect.

- Many people feel the most important aspect of a funeral is that it is an opportunity for people to say goodbye to a loved one, and also to support the family and friends of the person who has died.

- When the coffin or ashes are buried, the priest or vicar reminds people that we came from the ground when Adam was created, and return to the ground at death:

> We commit this body to the ground, earth to earth, ashes to ashes, dust to dust.

- This also reminds people the body is unimportant, it is the person's soul that lives on in the afterlife.

Q Explain why it might be more appropriate if people wore white clothes at a funeral, rather than black.

1 Why do many people wear black clothes at a funeral?

2 What is important about the phrase: 'We commit this body to the ground, earth to earth, ashes to ashes, dust to dust.'?

When writing about funerals, remember they are a sign of respect for the dead person, and also that Christians believe the person's soul has already left their body.

Life after death

➤ Christians believe that when they die they will have the chance of eternal life.

➤ Many Christians believe they may go to heaven, hell or purgatory, depending on how well they have lived on earth.

The central Christian belief is that the sacrifice of Jesus on the cross means all people who follow him will have the opportunity of eternal life with God when they die.

- This belief is found in the Nicene Creed where it states:

  We look for the resurrection of the dead, and the life of the world to come.

- It is not clear whether people will go straight to heaven after death, or whether they will wait until the Day of Judgement.

  Heaven is viewed as a paradise where people will live with God.

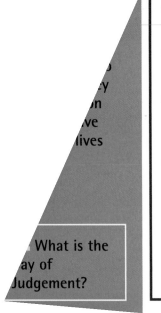

What is the Day of Judgement?

- People who have not lived a good life on earth will be sent to hell.

- Christian teaching and opinions about hell have changed over time.

- At one time, hell was believed to be a place of fire and brimstone, where people would be eternally punished by the devil.

- Today, many people think hell is simply a place where people are forever deprived from seeing God and being happy. In the same way, they see heaven as being eternally in the sight of God.

- Roman Catholics believe there is a place between heaven and hell called purgatory. Most Catholics are probably not good enough to go straight to heaven because of the sins they have committed on earth, but they have believed in Jesus so they will not go to hell. Instead, they are taken to purgatory where they are punished for a period of time before they are able to enter heaven.

- In 1999, Pope John Paul II described purgatory like this:

> 'Before we enter into God's Kingdom, every trace of sin within us must be eliminated, every imperfection in our soul corrected. This is exactly what takes place in purgatory.'

- He said that purgatory wasn't a physical place, but a state of being.

- The Bible is not clear about whether this new life after death is a physical or spiritual one. Some people believe they will be in heaven in their physical bodies, as they were on earth, while others believe it is just their souls which live on for eternity.

- **The Apostles' Creed** says:

> I believe... the resurrection of the body, and the life everlasting.

1 What does the Bible say about life after death?

2 Why do you think some people believe in purgatory?

> It is very important to remember that Christians do not believe in reincarnation. They believe that when you die you go to heaven, hell or, perhaps, purgatory. They do not believe that people's souls come back in another person.

The Christian year

➤ The year follows the life of Jesus.

➤ The year begins at Advent with the four week preparation for the birth of Jesus at Christmas.

A The Christian year

KEY FACTS

The Christian year follows the life of Jesus, beginning with Advent.

For Christians, Easter is a more important date than Christmas because this is when Jesus sacrificed his own life to save the people of the world.

Remember
Although some days, such as Christmas, happen on the same date each year, other Christian festivals fall at different times.

Following **Advent** is Christmas Day on 25 December.

The season of Christmas ends with **Epiphany** on 6 January. This festival remembers the visit of the wise men and the gifts they brought to Jesus. In the Eastern Churches Epiphany also remembers the baptism of Jesus.

Q What are the main parts of the Christian year?

Lent is the six weeks of preparation for Easter.

The Sunday before Easter is **Palm Sunday** when Jesus entered Jerusalem.

Remember
Advent is the beginning of the Christian year.

The period from Palm Sunday to **Easter Sunday** is **Holy Week**, remembering the last days of Jesus' life on earth.

A

Forty days after Easter is **Ascension Day** which commemorates the moment Jesus ascended into heaven.

Ten days later is **Pentecost** (Whitsun), the occasion which marks the coming of the Holy Spirit to the disciples.

During the Church's year there are also many **Saints' Days** and other holy days.

Some people used to begin the year on March 23rd – **Lady Day** – the day when Mary became pregnant.

Q Why did some people start the year on March 23rd?

1 Explain why Easter is more important than Christmas.

2 What benefits are there in having a yearly cycle of festivals?

There are several important days in the Christian year as well as Christmas and Easter and you should mention these in the exam, explaining why they are important.

THE BARE BONES
➤ Advent is the four week period leading up to Christmas.
➤ Christmas is the birthday of Christ.

A   What is Advent?

- Advent is the four week period leading up to Christmas. It begins on St Andrew's Day, November 30th, or the nearest Sunday to this.

> KEY FACT

> The word Advent means 'arrival', and Advent is a period of preparation for the celebration of the birth, or incarnation, of Jesus at Christmas.

- Advent marks the beginning of the Church's year.

- Advent is a solemn season, and in the past it was celebrated in the same way as Lent, with fasting and penitence.

- One of the customs associated with Advent is making Advent wreaths. These are rings of evergreens such as holly and ivy, with four red candles in them. One candle is lit on each Sunday of Advent until, at Christmas, all four are burning.

Remember
...son of ...istmas begins ...n Advent, a ...e for ...eparation, and ...nds with the ...isit of the Wise Men at Epiphany.

B   What is Christmas?

- Christmas is one of the most important festivals of the Christian year.

> EY FACT

> Christmas celebrates the incarnation, when God came to earth in human form. No-one actually knows exactly when Jesus was born, and it is more likely to have been in spring than in winter.

- The date of Christmas was fixed by Pope Gregory as late as 354 CE. Christmas was placed at this time to absorb existing pagan festivals of the winter solstice on 21st December. It also incorporated the Roman festival of Saturnalia and the northern European Yule festival.

- The practice of putting models of the manger in churches was started by St Francis of Assisi.

Who fixed
e date of
istmas?

c More about Christmas

Remember
Many of the things we associate with Christmas such as holly and ivy and yule logs are much older pagan rituals.

Q What pagan rituals are associated with Christmas?

EY FACT

• The practice of giving presents has two origins. The festival of St Nicholas, the patron saint of children takes place on 6th December, while the visit of the wise men to Bethlehem is celebrated by the church on January 6th (Epiphany). Most Christians, however, send cards and give presents at Christmas.

Advent and Christmas are vitally important because they mark the time when God chose to take the form of a human being and come to earth. This is called the 'incarnation'.

PRACTICE

1 Explain what is meant by the incarnation.

2 Why is Christmas celebrated on December 25th?

When you are writing about Christmas remember the tradition of giving presents really belongs to St Nicholas' Day and to Epiphany.

Lent, Holy Week and Easter

THE BARE BONES

➤ Lent encompasses the six weeks of preparation which lead up to Easter. It also recalls the time Jesus spent in the desert when he was tempted by the Devil.

➤ Easter is the most important festival in the whole of the Christian year, because it celebrates the resurrection of Jesus from the dead on Easter Sunday.

A Why is Lent important?

KEY FACT

During Lent Christians try to make themselves stronger against temptation, and prepare themselves for the celebration of Easter.

Remember
Lent is a time of preparation when people try to improve their lives.

- **Shrove Tuesday** is the last day before Lent begins. Traditionally people ate pancakes to use up luxury items such as eggs and butter before fasting.

- Lent begins with **Ash Wednesday**. Crosses made out of palm leaves for Palm Sunday are burnt and the ashes are used to make the sign of the cross on people's foreheads when they go to church. This shows that they are sorry for the things they have done wrong.

Q Why is Lent still an important time for Christians?

- In the past, Christians used to give up fish and meat entirely during Lent. Today, most Christians do not fast strictly, but **many give up a luxury** such as alcohol or sweets. This is a reminder of the sacrifice and death of Jesus.

B Why is Easter important?

- The week before Easter is **Holy Week** and recalls the last week Jesus spent in Jerusalem.

- According to the gospel writers, on the first Easter Sunday morning, women went to the tomb where Jesus had been buried. The women carried spices in order to anoint Jesus' body. When they got to the tomb, they found the stone across the entrance had been rolled away, and the tomb was empty. They were told that Jesus had been raised from the dead.

Remember
Easter proves to Christians that Jesus was the Son of God because he came back from the dead.

The resurrection is important, because for Christians it proves Jesus really was the Son of God, and has power over death.

KEY FACT

- Christians believe it shows that they, too, will have life after death.

c More about Easter

- Easter is not always on the same date every year. It falls on the first Sunday after the first full moon after the Spring equinox.

- On Easter Sunday morning, the church bells are rung. The church is decorated with flowers and candles, which were put away during Lent, and the atmosphere of the service is one of celebration. In some countries, there are processions and parades.

KEY FACT

Easter celebrates the death and resurrection of Jesus, when he overcame the power of death so that people could have eternal life.

1 Explain why Easter is so important to Christians.

2 Why do people sometimes give things up for Lent?

When you are writing about Lent and Easter remember that Lent begins with Ash Wednesday and Holy Week is the week before Easter, starting on Palm Sunday when Jesus rode into Jerusalem on a donkey.

THE BARE BONES
➤ Ascension Day is the day Jesus was taken up into heaven.
➤ Pentecost is the day when the apostles received the Holy Spirit.

A *What is Ascension day?*

Ascension Day is celebrated on the Thursday which falls forty days after Easter Sunday.

It commemorates Jesus' ascension, when he was taken up into heaven.

- After Jesus had been raised from the dead, according to the Bible, he met with his disciples and other followers. He ate and talked with them, until he was taken up into heaven. Jesus did not return to earth again.

- On one occasion, while he was eating with them, he gave them this command:

'Do not leave Jerusalem, but wait for the gift my Father promised, which you have heard me speak about. For John baptised with water, but in a few days you will be baptised with the Holy Spirit.' So when they met together, they asked him, 'Lord, are you at this time going to restore the kingdom to Israel?' He said to them: 'It is not for you to know the times or dates the Father has set by his own authority. But you will receive power when the Holy Spirit comes on you; and you will be my witnesses in Jerusalem, and in all Judea and Samaria, and to the ends of the earth.' After he said this, he was taken up before their very eyes, and a cloud hid him from their sight. (Acts 1:4-9)

- In some churches, special services are held on Ascension Day. In the past, people used to have the day off work so that they could go to church, but today, Ascension Day is often treated as a normal working day rather than a holiday.

Q What did Jesus say would happen in a few days time?

B What is Pentecost?

Pentecost is a Jewish festival called Shavuot which takes place seven weeks after Passover.

In Christianity, Pentecost is important because it was at the celebration of this festival that Christians first received the Holy Spirit – according to the Acts of the Apostles – appearing as tongues of flame over them.

Pentecost is celebrated on a Sunday seven weeks after Easter.

When the day of Pentecost came, they were all together in one place. Suddenly a sound like the blowing of a violent wind came from heaven and filled the whole house where they were sitting. They saw what seemed to be tongues of fire that separated and came to rest on each of them. All of them were filled with the Holy Spirit and began to speak in other tongues as the Spirit enabled them. Acts 2:1-4

- Pentecost is also known as 'Whitsun' or 'White Sunday' because of the white clothes that many people used to wear.

- Pentecost or Whitsun is known as the birthday of the church, because once the first Christians had the power of the Holy Spirit they were able to spread the message of Christianity.

- Pentecost is traditionally a day for baptisms. People often dress in white to represent purity. In some communities, it is a tradition to take part in walks as a demonstration of faith.

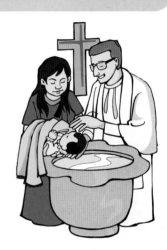

Ascension and Pentecost are two very important events because they mark the beginning of the Christian church.

1 What does Ascension Day celebrate?

2 On what day of the week is Ascension Day?

3 On what day of the week is Pentecost?

4 Why is Pentecost also known as Whitsun?

5 Why is Pentecost known as the birthday of the Church?

6 In which book of the Bible is the story of how the Holy Spirit was received at Pentecost found?

Remember, before his ascension Jesus promised his disciples that the Holy Spirit would come to them and this happened at Pentecost.

Caring for the poor

THE BARE BONES

➤ The Bible teaches that all Christians have a responsibility to care for the poor. Christians believe God will judge them according to how much concern they have shown for the poor.

➤ All the Christian churches today emphasise the need for people to share what they have with developing countries.

A   The prophet Amos

KEY FACTS

The Bible teaches that caring for the poor is one of the most important aspects of showing love for God.

- The prophet Amos lived in the eighth century BCE. The book of Amos is found in the Old Testament.

Amos preached a message of social justice.

- He warned the people that God would send terrible punishments unless they treated the poor and the weak with more care.

- Amos taught that God is not interested in listening to worship, if the people are ignoring the poor.

Q Was the prophet Amos preaching before, or after, the time of Jesus?

B   The parable of the sheep and goats

EY FACT

A parable is a story told to make a moral or religious point.

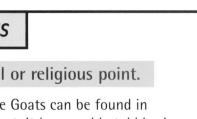

- The parable of the Sheep and the Goats can be found in Matthew 25, in the New Testament. It is a parable told by Jesus.

- It explains how God will judge people and separate them in the same way a farmer separates sheep from goats.

- Some people will be rewarded, because they have fed the hungry, given clothes to the needy, visited the sick and welcomed strangers. They will be by God's side for eternity.

- Other people will be punished, because they have done none of these things, and have ignored people in need.

Q What is a parable?

Jesus explained that when people care for each other, it is the same as caring for him. Christians believe showing love towards God involves caring about all other people.

Y FACT

C The story of the rich man and Lazarus

Q What is the main point of the story of the rich man and Lazarus?

- The story of the rich man and Lazarus is found in Luke 16:19-31. It is another example of a parable.

- It tells the story of a rich man who lived in luxury, while a beggar who lived outside his front gate had nothing and was ignored by the rich man. When the two men die, the poor man goes to heaven but the rich man is sent to hell. The rich man asks to be allowed to warn his brothers of the consequences of ignoring the poor, but he is told that they have had plenty of warnings already, from the prophets.

KEY FACT

> The parable teaches that people have been told for centuries that they must not ignore the poor, and they have no excuses.

D The principal of agape

Remember
There are many different Biblical passages that you could use in an answer about why Christians should care for the poor. Try and remember some key phrases, such as 'Always treat others as you would like to be treated yourself.'

- Jesus preached that people should show their love for God by being loving towards their neighbours. By 'neighbours', he meant everyone, even strangers or enemies. He taught that Christians should treat others the way they would like to be treated themselves. This unconditional love is called 'agape'.

- Christians should empathise with the poor. They should treat the poor in the way that they would like to be treated if they were poor. Giving should be generous, frequent, and done in a way that preserves the dignity of those less fortunate.

1 Explain Biblical teaching that might be used in a discussion about world poverty.

2 'If people do nothing to help the poor, they should not say they are Christians.' Do you agree? Give reasons to support your answer, and show you have thought about different points of view.

> If you can use quotations from the Bible to emphasise your points, it will help; but if you can't remember the exact words, you can still make general references to the text.

Christian aid agencies

THE BARE BONES

➤ There are many different aid agencies set up by Christians to try and put Christian ideas about care for the poor into practice.

➤ Some of the best known are Christian Aid, CAFOD and Tearfund.

A Christian Aid

KEY FACTS

Supporting aid agencies is a way in which Christians can put into practice their beliefs about the need to show concern for the poor.

Christian Aid is the overseas aid agency representing the World Council of Churches.

- It was set up after the Second World War in an attempt to help refugees in Europe, but it quickly expanded to provide aid for other countries too, particularly the poor in Africa.

- Christian Aid aims to provide help for people in times of emergencies, and is also involved in longer-term projects such as literacy programmes and education about AIDS.

- Christian Aid Week is a major fund-raising event held every year in May, when there are newspaper and television advertisements, street collections and envelopes delivered to houses.

Christian Aid
We believe in life before death

Q What is Christian Aid Week?

B Tearfund

KEY FACT

Tearfund is an organisation from the evangelical churches.

- It is a relief and development charity, which means it provides relief in emergencies and helps towards long-term development.

- It sends volunteers into refugee camps to help provide food and medical care in times of war and disaster.

Tearfund aims to teach people skills so they can become independent and not have to rely on charity.

Q Why do aid agencies try to give long-term aid, as well as helping out in emergencies?

KEY FACT

TEARFUND
CHRISTIAN ACTION WITH THE WORLD'S POOR

C CAFOD

IT'S TIME FOR JUSTICE
CAFOD

- CAFOD is the **overseas development and relief agency** of the Catholic Church in England and Wales, and is part of an international Catholic network called Caritas.

- CAFOD works with people in the third world to **tackle poverty and promote justice**, and helps them get access to the resources they need to become self-reliant.

- CAFOD also helps people in England and Wales to understand the causes of third world poverty, and **challenges the government and international organisations** through campaigns to make sure their policies benefit people living in poverty.

- CAFOD works with people regardless of their religion, ethnic origin, gender or politics.

Q Why does CAFOD use fasting as a method of fund-raising?

D Helping the poor

- There are many aid agencies. Some are Christian, some are affiliated to other religions, and many have no religious background at all. Lots of people think it is important to help the poor, whether they are religious or not.

- For Christians, helping the poor is an important part of faith. They believe it is not possible to love God if you ignore the needs of other human beings. They support aid agencies as a way of serving God, and to show they believe every person is valuable to God. They remember that Jesus cared for the poor, and they try to follow his example.

> If a question asks about a Christian aid agency, you should choose one that is explicitly Christian, rather than something like Oxfam which is not affiliated to any particular religious group.

Remember
When you are writing about Christian aid agencies, try to show how their work relates to Christian beliefs, rather than just describing what they do.

1 Describe the work of one Christian aid agency.

2 Explain why Christians might choose to support an overseas aid agency.

THE BARE BONES
➤ Christians believe greed for money can often prevent people from having a proper relationship with God.
➤ They believe the rich should share what they have with the poor.

A Biblical teaching about poverty and wealth

The Bible teaches that people who are rich and who care too much about their possessions should sell what they have and give the money to the poor; otherwise they will never be able to have a proper relationship with God.

KEY FACT

...mber
...asked
...t and
...des
...y,

Blessed are you who are poor, for yours is the kingdom of God. (Luke 6:20) Jesus told the poor they were special to God.

On the first day of every week, each of you is to put aside and save whatever extra you earn... (1 Corinthians 16:2) Paul told the early Christians to make a habit of setting aside some money out of their wages for the poor.

He looked up and saw rich people putting their gifts into the treasury; he also saw a poor widow put in two small copper coins. He said, 'Truly I tell you, this poor widow has put in more than all of them; for all of them have contributed out of their abundance, but she out of her poverty has put in all she had to live on.' (Luke 21:1-4) Jesus said that the amount of a gift was not as important as the generosity of the giver.

No-one can serve two masters; for a slave will either hate the one and love the other, or be devoted to the one and despise the other. You cannot serve God and wealth. (Matthew 6:24) Jesus said it is impossible to be ruled by God and by money at the same time.

The love of money is the root of all evil. (1 Timothy 6:10) All of the evil in the world comes about because of greed for money.

'You lack one thing: go, sell what you own, and give the money to the poor, and you will have treasure in heaven; then come, follow me.' When he heard this, he was shocked and went away grieving, for he had many possessions. (Mark 10:21-22) Jesus told a rich young man that if he was really serious about his faith, he should sell his possessions and give his money to the poor.

...o you
...ee that the
...ve of money
...s the root of
all evil?

b Earning money

Christians believe money should be earned fairly and honestly.

- Christians believe it is fine to work hard and earn money, as long as the work is honest, and the money doesn't take over the person's life.

- Christians do not usually approve of occupations which exploit other people or cause harm, such as gambling, pornography or promoting tobacco.

- Sometimes Christians try to choose jobs which involve helping others, such as nursing, the police, or charity work.

 What might a Christian think was a right or a wrong occupation to choose as a career?

c The church and wealth

 Why do some people think it is wrong for the Church to own expensive things?

Sometimes Christian churches are criticised for owning land, expensive buildings and treasures such as silver chalices. Some people think Christians should sell all this and give away the money to the poor and the homeless.

Others say that it is important to show respect to God with beautiful things, and that the churches need money in order to provide people with a place of worship and properly trained ministers.

---

1 Explain Biblical teachings about the use of wealth.

2 Describe how Christians might put their beliefs about the right use of money into practice in their daily lives.

3 'If people earn their money honestly, they should be free to spend it how they like.' Do you agree? Give reasons to support your answer, and show you have thought about different points of view. You must refer to Christianity in your answer.

The sanctity of life

THE BARE BONES

➤ Christians believe human life is sacred or holy.

➤ They believe all people are made in 'the image of God' as described in Genesis, which means, in a mysterious way, all people share something of the nature of God.

➤ Many Christians believe, because life is sacred, it should never deliberately be taken away.

A Christian belief

KEY FACT

Christians believe when God created people, he gave them something special, setting them apart from other animals.

> 'So God created man in his own image,
> In the image of God he created him;
> Male and female he created them.'
> (Genesis 1:27)

> 'The Lord God formed the man from the dust of the ground and breathed into his nostrils the breath of life, and the man became a living being.'
> (Genesis 2:7)

KEY FACT

Human life is different, holy and sacred. 'The sanctity of life' means the same as 'the holiness of life'.

Q What does Genesis teach about the sanctity of human life?

B The sanctity of life in practice

KEY FACT

Because Christians believe life is sacred, it can affect their attitudes towards all sorts of moral issues.

1 Abortion: if Christians believe life is sacred, even before it's born, they are likely to disagree with abortion and think it's the same as murder.

2 Euthanasia: believing in the sanctity of life is likely to make Christians think that euthanasia can't be justified.

3 Suicide: if Christians believe that lives are sacred, they are not likely to choose to end their own lives, although suicides often happen when people have gone beyond the point of being able to make a careful decision.

4 Capital punishment: if Christians believe human life is sacred, then they might think it can never be right to kill someone, even if that person has committed very serious crimes.

5 Fighting in war: some Christians believe, because human life is sacred, it can never be right to kill another person, even in war-time.

Q Can you explain your own views about these issues, with reasons?

C Different Christian views

- Some Christians believe that although life is sacred, it can still be ended in some circumstances. They believe the most important principle is love. They say it can sometimes be right to take away life, if it is the most loving thing to do, for example if someone is in a lot of pain and wants their own death to come more quickly, or if a pregnancy is likely to result in the birth of a severely disabled baby. They say decisions like these still respect the sanctity of life

When you are writing about any moral issues involving life and death, you can include ideas about the sanctity of life to show that you understand why Christians feel strongly about this.

D The image of God

- When the Bible says people are made 'in the image of God', it is not entirely clear what this means. Christians have often interpreted it to mean that humans share something of God's nature.

- Christians believe people have souls. They believe the soul is a part of a person which is separate from the body. When the body dies, the soul does not die with it, but continues to live after death. The soul is the part of the person that joins God in heaven and lasts for ever.

- Christians believe the soul sets people apart from other animals. It makes human life different from all other forms of life.

- Many Christians believe people have souls even before they are born, while they are growing during pregnancy.

1 Explain what Christians mean when they say life is sacred.

2 How might belief in the sanctity of life affect a Christian's attitude towards abortion?

3 'If life is holy, we should be allowed to end it when people are in pain.' Do you agree? Give reasons to support your answer, and show you have thought about different points of view. You must refer to Christianity in your answer.

Contraception (birth control)

THE BARE BONES

➤ Contraception, or birth control, is about deliberately preventing pregnancy, or planning pregnancy.

➤ Many Christians think using contraception is sensible and responsible. Others, particularly Roman Catholics, believe artificial contraception goes against God's plans.

A What is contraception?

KEY FACT

When people talk about contraception, or birth control, they are referring to deliberate, natural and artificial ways of preventing pregnancy.

Q What reasons might a Christian give in favour of the use of contraception?

- There are many different forms of contraception, such as the Pill, condoms, and 'the coil' (inter-uterine devices). They prevent conception in different ways. Some work better than others, but most of the artificial methods are very effective.

- Natural methods of contraception, such as limiting sex to times in the month when a woman is less fertile, still allow for the possibility of pregnancy.

KEY FACT

Christians disagree about whether it is right to use contraception. Some think artificial contraceptives should not be used because God might want a couple to have a baby. Other Christians think using contraception is part of a responsible sexual relationship.

B Why do people use contraception?

They might use condoms in order to avoid sexually transmitted diseases.

They might be in a sexual relationship but not want children at this stage.

They might want to choose the age gap between their children.

Different reasons for people to use contraception.

They might not be in a committed relationship.

They might already have as many children as they want.

They might not want to have children at all.

c What do Christians think about contraception?

Q How are Roman Catholic views different from the views of other churches?

Remember
You need to explain why people hold their opinions. You might refer to beliefs about God planning each person, or beliefs about the sanctity of life.

The **Roman Catholic Church** believes people should not interfere with **Natural Law**; it teaches that God made sex for the purpose of **reproduction**, and people should not go against God's purposes. Roman Catholics usually believe only natural methods of contraception are acceptable, but there should always be the possibility of pregnancy, in case God plans for a child to be born.

The **Church of England** and the **Methodist Church** teach that contraception is an acceptable way of preventing unwanted pregnancies. These churches encourage people to make **responsible choices** about the size of families. Many other churches agree with this too.

Remember in your answer to concentrate on the religious ideas, rather than, for example, explaining how the contraception works.

1 Describe, and explain, different Christian attitudes towards contraception (birth control).

2 'A married couple should be prepared to have as many children as God wants to give them.' Do you agree? Give reasons to support your answer, and show you have thought about different points of view. You must refer to Christianity in your answer.

THE BARE BONES

➤ Fertility treatment helps people to have babies when they aren't able to conceive naturally.

➤ Embryo research uses human embryos for experiments, to find out new ways of curing illnesses and preventing disability.

➤ Christians sometimes object to both of these, especially if they think human life begins as soon as an egg is fertilised.

A   What is fertility treatment?

KEY FACT

Fertility treatment is medical help given to people who want to have babies but are unable to conceive naturally. Often, fertility treatment is not available on the National Health, and people have to pay for it.

There are several different fertility treatments available, and they do not always work.

What kinds of fertility treatment are available?

AIH is Artificial Insemination by Husband, when the egg and the sperm come from the couple who want to be parents, but medical help is needed for fertilisation to take place. Sometimes women who do not ovulate normally receive donor eggs from another woman.

AID is Artificial Insemination by Donor, when sperm is donated by an anonymous man.

IVF is In Vitro Fertilisation, where the egg and sperm are brought together for fertilisation in a laboratory rather than inside the woman's body. If embryos form, some or all of them are implanted in the woman's uterus in the hope that a successful pregnancy will result.

Remember
New techniques for fertility treatment and embryo research are developing all the time.

Q What are your own views about fertility treatment?

B   What do Christians think about fertility treatment?

Some Christians, especially **Roman Catholics**, believe fertility treatment is wrong, because it **interferes with nature and with God's plan** for couples. They might say, if a couple can't conceive naturally, this is because God does not want them to become parents.

Other Christians believe fertility treatment is often a good thing, because it helps to bring **new life** into the world and gives **happiness** to the people who want to be parents.

K...
Many...
think life...
at the...
of...

B

Christians often express **doubts about some aspects** of fertility treatments, even if they believe, on the whole, they are a good thing:

1 They might object to the creation of 'spare embryos' during IVF, which are sometimes destroyed or used for medical research. They might argue that an embryo is still a human life.

2 They might object to the use of eggs or sperm from anonymous donors, because they might think this is similar to adultery.

3 They might object to fertility treatments being made available for people who are not married, homosexual or past the age for child-bearing, because this might not be the way God intended things to happen.

Q Why do some Christians have doubts about fertility treatment?

C What do Christians think about embryo research?

Christians believe life is sacred, and that this should be respected whenever decisions are made about the beginnings of a new human life.

What is embryo research?

- Embryo research involves the study and use of human embryos in order to find ways of preventing or curing illnesses and disabilities, such as Parkinson's disease and Motor Neurone Disease.

- Human tissue from embryos can be implanted into living patients to slow down serious diseases of the nervous system. This embryo tissue usually comes from abortions.

Some Christians think embryo research is acceptable, because it means some good can come out of an abortion, even if the abortion itself was not a good action. The human tissue used to treat illnesses of the nervous system often works very well, much better than ordinary drugs. They say that **Jesus was a healer**, and that embryo research can be a good way of bringing healing or preventing illness.

Others think it is wrong to use human tissue in this way, because it is treating human life as **'a means to an end'**, rather than as valuable in its own right. The embryo cannot give consent to being used in this way.

EY FACT

Remember
The Bible does not say anything about fertility treatment or embryo research.

Q What are your own views about embryo research?

1 Explain why Christians might have different views about fertility treatment.

2 'Embryo research does such a lot of good that the problems it raises should be ignored.' Do you agree? Give reasons to support your answer, and show that you have thought about different points of view. You must refer to Christianity in your answer.

Abortion

THE BARE BONES

➤ Before a baby is born, while it is still developing in the uterus, it is called a foetus. In the very early stages of development, it is called an embryo.

➤ Abortion is when the life of an embryo or a foetus ends before the baby is born.

A What does the word 'abortion' mean?

KEY FACT

Doctors use the word 'abortion' to mean the ending of any pregnancy before a baby is born; this includes miscarriage, when the pregnancy ends naturally. But usually, when people talk about abortion, they mean pregnancies which are ended deliberately.

Many Christians are against abortion, because they believe God plans every human life even before birth, and they think abortion is **similar to murder**.

But some Christians disagree. Others believe in some situations, abortion might be **the kindest or the most sensible choice**.

Q Why do some Christians think abortion is similar to murder?

B Why do women sometimes have abortions?

Pregnant women might choose to have an abortion for a variety of reasons:

- Her mental or physical health might be at risk if she has the baby.

- She might be pregnant as the result of a rape.

- There might be a good reason to suspect, if the baby is born, it will have serious health problems.

The most common reason given for abortion is that the woman's mental health is at risk; she might feel unable to cope with a baby because she is very young, because she has no partner, because it would interfere with her career, or she might just feel that it is not the right time for her to have a baby.

Remember, although you might have your own strong views on a subject, you're meant to explain what Christians think too.

C Abortion and the law

1 If a woman wants an abortion, two doctors have to agree she wants it for a good reason.

2 The abortion must happen as early as possible in the pregnancy, before the foetus is 'viable' (before it could live outside the womb without medical help).

3 Abortion has been legal since 1967, and can be performed up to the twenty-fourth week of pregnancy, although abortions nearly always take place much earlier.

D Biblical teaching about God's plan

Q How might the belief that God has plans for each human life affect a Christian's attitude to abortion?

The Bible teaches that people are made 'in the image of God' (Genesis), and that God has a plan for every individual: 'Before I formed you in the womb I knew you, before you were born I set you apart.' (Jeremiah 1.5). Many Christians are against abortion, because they believe, even before the pregnancy is completed and the baby is born, God has a plan for the potential life.

E Differing points of view within Christianity

Remember
Even within one church, there will be people with a variety of views about abortion.

Q Which Christian church teaches that abortion is almost always wrong?

The Roman Catholic Church teaches that abortion is nearly always wrong. It is only allowed if it has to happen during an operation to save the mother's life, for example, if she has cancer of the uterus.

The Church of England teaches that abortion is a very serious issue and should not be chosen unless it is the last resort, but it can be allowed in some circumstances, and the final decision should be made by the people involved.

Other churches also teach that abortion is very serious, but sometimes necessary as a last resort. Some Christians believe there are times when abortion is the kindest thing, for example if the mother is very young, or if the foetus is developing abnormally and is likely to have serious health problems.

1 Explain Christian teaching which might be used in a discussion about abortion.

2 Explain why Christians might have different views about abortion.

3 'Abortion is the same as murder.' Do you agree? Give reasons to support your answer, and show you have thought about different points of view. You must refer to Christianity in your answer.

Euthanasia

> It is against the law in the UK to do anything deliberately to hasten someone else's death, even if they are in great pain and have asked to be helped to die.

> Most Christians disagree with euthanasia.

A Classifying euthanasia

The word 'euthanasia' comes from two Greek words, 'eu' which means 'good' and 'thanatos' which means 'death' – so 'euthanasia' means 'a good death'.

KEY FACT

Most Christians believe it is wrong to choose the time of your own death, and that this is best left to God.

Active euthanasia is when deliberate steps are taken to end someone's life, for example by giving a lethal injection.

Passive euthanasia is when treatment which would have helped the person to live longer is stopped, for example if the patient has a heart attack, they are not resuscitated.

Ways of classifying euthanasia

Involuntary euthanasia is when other people decide that the patient should die, for example if he or she is in a coma, or new-born, or unable to communicate.

Voluntary euthanasia is when someone asks to be given help to die, and makes it clear that this is his or her own choice.

Q What are the four different ways of classifying euthanasia?

B Church teaching on euthanasia

- The Roman Catholic Church teaches that life can only be ended by euthanasia if the dose of painkillers necessary to ease suffering is strong enough to kill the patient. The aim should be to stop the suffering, not to kill.

- Christians also accept it is not necessary to go to extraordinary lengths to keep someone alive if they have no hope of recovery.

Although you need to explain your own views, remember to leave enough time to describe Christian opinions and the reasons Christians hold them.

Q What does the Roman Catholic Church teach about euthanasia?

C Why some Christians are for euthanasia

Remember
The Bible doesn't say anything directly about euthanasia, because it was written before modern medicine made these things possible.

1 Christians say that in some situations, helping someone to die to end their pain is the most loving thing to do. The Bible teaches 'Always treat others as you would like to be treated yourself.' If you would prefer euthanasia rather than end your life in pain, then you should allow it for other people.

2 They might argue God has given us the ability to think for ourselves, and we should be allowed to make our own decisions about the right time to die.

3 They might argue that if we keep patients alive with drugs when they are very ill, this is going against God's wishes by preventing the death God wants.

D Why some Christians are against euthanasia

1 Many Christians are against euthanasia, because they believe life is a gift from God. They believe only God has the right to take life away, and that God will choose the right time for someone to die.

2 Many Christians believe suffering can bring people closer to God. If they are in pain, they might turn to God more than they would if they were fit and healthy. Suffering might help someone to understand the suffering of Jesus.

Q What do people mean when they talk about a 'slippery slope argument'?

3 Christians and other people sometimes argue, if euthanasia were legalised, that it would be open to abuse by some people. The elderly might be encouraged to die quickly by relatives wishing to avoid paying for their care, or to inherit money. People might try to disguise murder as euthanasia. This is sometimes called the 'slippery slope' argument, because once it starts, it is difficult to keep it under control.

4 Some Christians argue that hospices provide dying people with the chance to end their lives with dignity and without pain, so euthanasia should not be necessary.

1 Explain why Christians might disagree about whether euthanasia can ever be right.

2 Describe how a Christian might respond to a close relative with a terminal illness who expressed a wish to end his or her life.

3 'All life is worth having, even a life which is full of pain.' Do you agree? Give reasons to support your answer and show you have thought about different points of view. You must refer to Christianity in your answer.

The hospice movement

➤ Hospices are places where people who are terminally ill can go to live permanently, or for short breaks.

➤ Hospice staff try to help people to live with dignity and without pain until their lives come to a natural end.

A History of the hospice movement

KEY FACT

Some Christians believe there are better ways to help a person die with dignity than euthanasia. Hospices are nursing homes where people who are dying can be looked after by trained medical staff.

- The first hospices were started by Christians, as places of shelter for the poor and for travellers.

- The founder of the contemporary hospice movement was a Christian doctor called **Dame Cicely Saunders.** She was inspired to begin her work by a Polish patient she met, who was dying in pain and without the support of family and friends. She used to visit him in hospital and try to make him feel as though he was not alone. When he died, he left her some money to begin her first hospice.

- Cicely Saunders set up **St. Christopher's Hospice** in London in 1967.

- Today there are hospices all over the country. Some are especially for children.

Q Why do some people think life in a hospice is better than choosing euthanasia?

B What are hospices for?

- Hospices aim to provide places where people who are terminally ill can spend the ends of their lives, if they want to.

- They are also places where people who are normally cared for at home can go for a break, to give the carers a rest.

- Hospices give medical treatment to make dying people more comfortable.

- They provide counselling and support, to help patients and their families prepare for death.

- They often continue to support the family once the patient has died.

C Christianity and the hospice movement

Many hospices are run by Christians, as an alternative to euthanasia.

- However, hospices are not just for Christian patients, and not everyone who works in a hospice is a Christian.

- The staff in a hospice don't try to persuade the patients to believe in God, but there are services of worship and visits from ministers and priests for people who want them.

- Some people devote their lives to hospice work because of their Christian faith. They believe that all people have dignity and are made 'in the image of God', and that as Christians they should do all they can to treat dying patients in the way they would want to be treated themselves.

- Some people think hospices are a good alternative to euthanasia, because they give people the chance to say goodbye to their families and to end their lives as comfortably as is possible.

Remember
Christians might support the work of a hospice because they believe every human life is sacred, even if the life is coming to an end.

D Mother Teresa and hospices

- **Mother Teresa of Calcutta** was a nun who believed people should be allowed to die with dignity. She devoted her life to working amongst the poorest people of India. She was appalled to see some people dying at the side of the road, with no-one to care for them, and no privacy. Mother Teresa set up hospices in India where the dying could go to be made more comfortable, and where they could be made to feel that they mattered. **She taught that every human life was important to God.**

Q Why did Mother Teresa set up homes for the dying?

1 Who founded St Christopher's Hospice, and when?

2 Explain the main aims of hospices.

3 Explain how and why a Christian might support the work of a hospice.

Try not to get so carried away with historical background that you forget to mention religious ideas.

THE BARE BONES

➤ Christian opinion about fighting during war-time is divided.

➤ The Bible has teachings which suggest some wars are commanded by God, but it also says Christians should love their enemies. It can be used to support both sides of the argument.

A Biblical teaching that supports fighting in wars

- The Bible teaches that Christians should defend the weak, and should fight against evil.

- The Old Testament tells stories of God commanding the people to go to war.

> Proclaim this among the nations; prepare for war! (Joel 3:9)

This suggests God sometimes wants people to fight against enemies.

- Jesus once became violent when he saw how people were misusing the Temple.

> He overturned the tables of the money-changers and the benches of those selling doves. (Mark 11:15)

Christians might use this incident to show that Jesus thought it was acceptable to use violence in some circumstances.

- Jesus came into contact with soldiers, but the Gospels never suggest he thought they were wrong to do this job.

Q Some people say the Old Testament is full of war and fighting, while the New Testament is full of peace and love. Do you think this is a fair thing to say?

B Other reasons why Christians might support wars

- Many Christians believe it is right to fight for your country in times of war, because the enemy would otherwise win and evil would overcome good.

- Many Christians also believe fighting in a war can be a way of showing love, because soldiers are willing to risk their lives in order for their countrymen to live safely.

Q Can you think of any examples of wars or battles mentioned in the Bible?

C   The Just War

KEY FACT

A Just War is seen as a war which has to be fought but is conducted according to certain conditions.

- These conditions were first proposed by **Thomas Aquinas** (c. 1225–1274) and then expanded upon by **Francisco de Vitoria** (1483–1546). A war is just (or fair) only if these conditions are met:

1 The war must be declared by a proper authority, such as a government, and not by individual groups.

2 There must be a good reason for the war, which does not include greed.

3 The intention of the war must be to do good and not evil. Wars cannot be carried out for revenge or to intimidate people.

4 War must be a last resort, all other methods of solving the problem must have been tried first.

5 The war must do more good than harm.

6 It must be possible to win; if there is no hope of victory, lives should not be risked by going to war.

7 The methods used must be fair; the fighters should not use any more violence than is strictly necessary.

These conditions are designed to prevent war and to limit its effects.

Q Do you think the rules about a Just War could be useful today, or has war changed too much since their formation?

KEY FACT

D   Biblical teaching that opposes war and violence

At **the Sermon on the Mount,** Jesus said:

Blessed are the peacemakers.
(Matthew 5:9)

Love your enemies, and pray for those who persecute you.
(Matthew 5:44)

Jesus also said:

'Put your sword back in its place,' Jesus said to him, 'for all who draw the sword will die by the sword.'
(Matthew 26:52)

Remember
...Christians can use different texts to ...points of view.

1 Explain Biblical teaching which might be used in a discussion about war.

2 Describe Christian teaching about a Just War.

3 'It can never be right for a Christian to fight in a war.' Do you agree? Give reasons to support your answer, and show you have thought about different points of view.

Human rights

THE BARE BONES

➤ Christians believe all human beings are valuable, because they were made individually by God in his image.

➤ The Christian churches have all given their support to the United Nations Declaration of Human Rights.

A The UN declaration of human rights

- The United Nations made a statement saying what they thought basic human rights should be. This statement was made after the Second World War, while everyone still remembered the terrible things that had happened to Jews, prisoners of war, and people who had been attacked by nuclear weapons.

- The statement said:

KEY FACT

> Everyone should be treated equally and without prejudice, and that people should be able to expect a fair trial. No-one should be tortured or kept in prison without a good reason. People should be free to hold whatever opinions they think are right.

> For I was hungry and you gave me something to eat, I was thirsty and you gave me something to drink, I was a stranger and you invited me in, I needed clothes and you clothed me, I was sick and you looked after me, I was in prison and you came to visit me. (Matthew 25:35-36)

Q Why do Christians believe everyone should have the same basic human rights?

B Liberation theology

- Liberation theology began in the 1960s in Central and South America, mainly within the Roman Catholic Church.

KEY FACTS

> The movement believes that Christians have a duty to stand up and fight against poverty, oppression and injustice.

- In countries such as El Salvador, government corruption meant a few people were very rich while many were very poor. Those who protested against the government were often arrested, held without trial, tortured or just 'disappeared'.

> Liberation theologians argue that it is wrong for Christians to stand by and do nothing when people are being denied their basic human rights.

- Camilo Torres and Oscar Romero are examples of Roman Catholic priests who believed in Liberation Theology and were killed because of their beliefs.

- Other Christians believe Liberation Theology is too political, and that Christians should work and pray for peace.

Q What arguments might be used for or against Liberation Theology?

C Amnesty International

Remember
Amnesty International is not a Christian organisation, but Christians might support it because holds the belief that everyone is equally valuable to God.

Q What do you think the Amnesty International logo is meant to represent?

Christians might put their beliefs about human rights into action by supporting an organisation such as Amnesty International.

amnesty international

- Amnesty International is not a Christian organisation, but it aims to protect human rights. It began in 1961, when Peter Benenson, a British lawyer, read about some students who had been sent to prison unfairly.

Amnesty campaigns:

'to free all prisoners of conscience; ensure fair and prompt trials for political prisoners; abolish the death penalty, torture and other cruel treatment of prisoners; end political killings and "disappearances"; and oppose human rights abuses by opposition groups.'

- 'Prisoners of conscience' are people who are in prison because of their beliefs, whether or not they have committed any crime.

- Amnesty works by setting up letter-writing and publicity campaigns as well as protests so people are made aware of particular human rights abuses. Many countries who practice abuses do not wish the rest of the world to know what is going on and so may stop if they are exposed.

- Amnesty has over a million members in more than 160 countries.

1 Explain Biblical teaching which might be used in a discussion about human rights.

2 Explain why Christians might support the work of an organisation which supports basic human rights like Amnesty.

Read the question carefully: don't write too much about the history of an organisation if the question asks about its work.

Capital punishment

THE BARE BONES

➤ Capital punishment is the death penalty, when someone is killed as a punishment for his or her crimes.

➤ Some Christians are in favour of capital punishment, and others are against it; both sides of the argument can be supported by the Bible.

A The aims of punishment

- Christianity teaches that God is loving and forgiving and that Christians should try to love and forgive everyone, even their enemies. But this does not mean criminals should be allowed to get away with breaking the law.

- People usually say there are four main reasons for punishing criminals:

1 Deterrence – to stop other people from committing the same crime.

2 Retribution – to pay the criminal back for the crime.

3 Protection – to protect the rest of society from the criminal.

4 Reformation – to make the criminal into a better person.

- Some Christians devote time to working with criminals and try to help them turn away from crime.

- Although all the Christian churches would agree murder is wrong, they have different views about capital punishment.

B Why Christians might support capital punishment

- The Bible teaches there are some crimes which should be punished by death – 'a life for a life'.

> Show no pity: life for life, eye for eye, tooth for tooth, hand for hand, foot for foot. (Deuteronomy 19:21)

- The Bible teaches that the weak should be protected, and the death penalty might be seen as a way of protecting people against criminals.

- The death penalty ensures the criminal can never repeat the crimes; no one has to worry about what he or she might do when released.

- The death penalty might be seen as kinder than a life spent in prison.

- The public might feel justice has been done.

- The death penalty might deter other people from committing similar crimes.

Q If the death penalty were introduced for the most serious crimes, which crimes do you think would deserve it, if any?

KEY FACT

The UK stopped using capital punishment in 1965, but since then some people have tried to bring it back for particularly serious crimes.

C Why Christians might be against capital punishment

Remember
Christians disagree about the death penalty.

- The Bible teaches that people should be forgiving.

- The Bible also teaches that people should not kill.

- Someone would have to be an executioner, and this might have a damaging effect on him or her.

- The death penalty leaves no chance of the criminal ever becoming a better person.

- The family of the offender might suffer more than the criminal, even though they didn't commit the crime.

- Sometimes people have been executed and then it was discovered that they didn't commit the crime.

- At the Sermon on the Mount Jesus said:

> Do not judge, or you too will be judged. For in the same way as you judge others, you will be judged, and with the measure you use, it will be measured to you. (Matthew 7:1-2)

D Church views on capital punishment

- The Church of England believes the justice system must be merciful but should also show that wrongdoing will be punished. The General Synod of the Church said recently that any reintroduction of capital punishment would be 'deplored'.

- The Roman Catholic Church has never said officially that capital punishment is wrong, although many bishops have made statements condemning it.

- The Religious Society of Friends (Quakers) has always been totally opposed to capital punishment.

> A deep reverence for human life is worth more than a thousand executions in the prevention of murder; and is, in fact, the great security for human life. The law of capital punishment while pretending to support this reverence, does in fact tend to destroy it. (John Bright MP, 1868)

Q What do most of the

out

unish

1 Describe Christian teaching which might be used in a discussion about capital punishment.

2 'Capital punishment is the same as murder.' Do you agree? Give reasons to support your answer, and show you have thought about different points of view. You must refer to Christianity in your answer.

> Even if you feel very strongly about an issue, you must remember to refer to the religion you are studying.

Pacifism

THE BARE BONES

➤ Pacifists believe it is never right to use violence.

➤ They do not fight for their countries in times of war.

➤ They never use violence when they are protesting against something.

A What is pacifism?

Pacifism is the belief that it is desirable and possible to abolish war and violence.

- People who are pacifists recognise there are times when conflicts arise, but they believe the best way to deal with conflict is through **non-violent protest**, such as peaceful demonstrations, boycotts, and peaceful non-cooperation.

- During times of war, people who object to being soldiers are called **'conscientious objectors'**, which means their consciences tell them they must not fight. However, some conscientious objectors drive ambulances or do other 'non-combatant' duties in wartime.

- Pacifism can be applied at any time of conflict, whether or not there is a war. For example, Martin Luther King used peaceful methods of protest against racism during the Civil Rights Movement in the USA. He gave speeches and organised boycotts, marches and sit-ins to make his point that black people should have equal rights with white people.

Q Do you think pacifism shows bravery, or cowardice?

B   The Quakers (Religious Society of Friends)

EY FACT

The Society of Friends (Quakers) is a Christian church which is committed to pacifism. Some Christians, but not all, are pacifists.

- The Quaker movement started with George Fox in the seventeenth century. By 1660, Quakers had made a statement saying they would have nothing to do with war.

- Quakers believe the way to resolve conflicts is to use 'weapons of the spirit', such as love, truth and co-operation.

- During the First and Second World Wars, many Quakers were conscientious objectors. The Friends Ambulance Unit was run by pacifists, who did not fight but instead risked their lives by carrying the wounded from battles to hospitals.

C   Why are some Christians pacifists?

Remember
Not all Christians are pacifists, and not all pacifists are Christians.

- Some Christians believe the commandment 'Do not kill' includes all kinds of killing, even if it is in war-time.

- Christians believe all human beings are created by God 'in his own image', and some believe it can never be right to use violence against others.

- The Bible praises the peace-makers. Jesus tells people to 'turn the other cheek' if they are attacked, and to love their enemies. Many Christians believe it is not possible to love an enemy and kill the enemy at the same time.

- Some Christians join movements such as the Campaign for Nuclear Disarmament, because of their belief that violence can never be right.

EY FACT

Jesus is often described as a pacifist.

- Many pacifist Christians base their views on Jesus' teachings about love.

Q Which Biblical teachings might a Christian use to support pacifism?

A new command I give you: Love one another. As I have loved you, so you must love one another.
(John 13:34)

But I tell you: Love your enemies and pray for those who persecute you, that you may be sons of your Father in heaven.
(Matthew 5:44)

1 Explain why some Christians believe it can never be right to fight in a war.

2 Describe how Christians might put their beliefs about peace into action in their daily lives.

Try to use the right terminology in your answers. Show you understand key vocabulary by using words like 'pacifism' and 'conscientious objector'.

Prejudice

THE BARE BONES
➤ Prejudice is a preconceived opinion or bias, usually <u>against</u> a person or a thing.
➤ Prejudice is usually based on lack of knowledge.

A Prejudice and the law

1 People are discriminated against (treated unfairly) for a variety of reasons: because of **race** and **religion**, because of **gender**, because of **sexuality**, because of **physical appearance** and **ability**, because of **age**. Most kinds of discrimination are against the law, but they still happen.

2 The **Universal Declaration of Human Rights** made by the United Nations in 1948 stated that everyone has the same human rights regardless of race, colour, sex or religion.

3 In 1975, the **Sex Discrimination Act** was passed to protect men and women against discrimination on the basis of gender, and in 1976 the Race Relations Act made it illegal to discriminate against people because of their race.

> Prejudice and discrimination have existed throughout history. For example, racial prejudice has led to the slave trade, apartheid, the Holocaust and 'ethnic cleansing'; religious prejudice causes problems in Northern Ireland.

Q What sorts of people are sometimes the victims of prejudice?

B Biblical teaching about equality

• The Old Testament teaches that all people are to be treated with respect and care. It gives laws about how people should behave towards immigrants:

> 'Do not ill-treat foreigners who are living in your land.' (Leviticus 19:33).

The laws tell people they must give everyone the same opportunities and the same pay for a fair day's work.

• The New Testament teaches that Christian faith breaks down barriers between people.

> 'There is no longer Jew or Greek, there is no longer slave or free, there is no longer male or female; for all of you are one in Christ Jesus.'(Galatians 3:28).

Q How might a Christian put into action his or her beliefs that prejudice is wrong?

C   The parable of the Good Samaritan

- This parable was told by Jesus – a traveller was robbed and injured and left at the side of the road. Three respectable Jews went past and saw him but didn't want to get involved with helping him. A Samaritan, who was from a different race and usually treated with prejudice, stopped and helped the man who was injured.

EY FACT

> Jesus told this parable to show that people should treat everyone else as neighbours, whatever their ethnic origin.

D   Christians and racism

EY FACT

> Christian teaching says racism is never justified. All people are equally valuable to God and should be treated equally.

> Apartheid: Before 1990 the laws of South Africa were racist. Black and white people were kept apart, and black people had to live in poor housing with very few rights and no voice. If they protested, they were dealt with violently.

- Even though the Bible teaches that racism is wrong, Christianity does not have a very good record in the struggle for equal rights. Some Christians in the past were enthusiastic slave owners. Even today, black people are under-represented in Christian leadership.

- Some Christians devote their lives to making the world a fairer place for all races. There are many ways in which Christians could put their beliefs about equality into action, such as joining **anti-racist organisations**, making members of ethnic minorities feel welcome in the community, and making sure **equal opportunities** policies are acted upon at work. Martin Luther King, Desmond Tutu and Trevor Huddleston are examples of Christians who have devoted their lives to a struggle against racism.

Q How might the Parable of the Good Samaritan be used in a discussion about racism?

Remember
There is nothing in the New Test...ent which ...... racial

1 Explain Biblical teaching which might be used in a discussion about racism.

2 Describe how Christians might put their beliefs about racial equality into practice in their daily lives.

In the exam, make references to teachings such as the parable of the Good Samaritan, but don't waste time telling the whole story in detail.

The struggle against racism

THE BARE BONES

➤ Martin Luther King and Trevor Huddleston are both examples of Christians who have worked in the fight against racism.

➤ Because of their Christian beliefs that all people are made 'in the image of God', they have tried to get equal rights for everyone and to bring an end to racist laws.

A Martin Luther King

KEY FACT

> Some Christians have given up their whole lives to the struggle against racism, because of their belief that all people are equally valuable to God.

Remember
When you are writing about people who have worked against racism or other kinds of unfairness, you need to mention their Christian beliefs. Explain what encouraged them to do this work.

1929 — Martin Luther King was a black American Christian who believed God created black and white people as equally valuable, made 'in the image of God'.

He lived in America from 1929 to 1968, at a time when it was not against the law to discriminate against black people. Black people were often not allowed to use public facilities such as parks, cinemas and swimming pools.

Because of his Christian beliefs, Martin Luther King worked towards equality by organising non-violent protests. He believed it could never be right to use violence, because this does not express the love of God, only hatred.

He campaigned against black and white people having separate seats on buses, separate schools and separate restaurants. He organised freedom marches and gave speeches protesting against injustice.

Martin Luther King's most famous speech told of his dream that one day all races would live peacefully together and treat each other with respect.

Q Why did Martin Luther King refuse to use violence?

1968 — Dr King was awarded the Nobel Peace Prize in 1964. In April 1968, he was shot dead, but others carried on his work.

B

- Martin Luther King fought for the **rights of black Americans** because he believed God created **everyone to be equal** and to live together peacefully.

> I have a dream that my four little children will one day live in a nation where they will not be judged by the colour of their skin but by the content of their character. I have a dream today! (Martin Luther King)

C *Trevor Huddleston*

Trevor Huddleston was an Anglican Archbishop who spent many years of his life working in South Africa, standing up for the victims of apartheid. | 1913

Because of his Christian beliefs, he thought it was wrong for black people to be treated as inferior to white.

He believed Christians have a duty to stand up for people who are being treated unfairly. It is wrong to stand back and do nothing.

Trevor Huddleston led the British Movement against Apartheid, and said it was impossible to be a Christian if you did nothing about injustice.

He encouraged people around the world to refuse to play sports against South African teams until South Africa stopped using the system of apartheid. He encouraged people to stop buying South African goods such as apples and wine.

He became friends with many other people in South Africa who also worked to abolish apartheid, such as Oliver Tambo and Desmond Tutu.

Trevor Huddleston died in 1998, but he had lived long enough to see the ending of apartheid in South Africa. | 1998

Q What did Trevor Huddleston encourage people around the world to do, to show South Africa that they disapproved of apartheid?

1 Explain how and why one well-known Christian has tried to make the world a fairer place for all races.

2 'Christians should always fight against racism.' Do you agree? Give reasons to support your answer, and show you have thought about different points of view.

> If asked to describe the work of a well-known Christian, make sure the person you choose is a Christian!

Family

> ➤ The Christian marriage service often stresses one of the reasons for getting married is so that a couple can have children and bring them up in the Christian faith.
> ➤ Many Christians believe the family has an important part to play in religious life.

A The role of the Christian family

KEY FACT

Christians believe family members have duties towards one another.

Families are often in a good position to offer hospitality and to make newcomers feel welcome.

Families can bring up the next generation to follow the Christian faith and continue the work of the church.

Q What do you think parents might do to try and bring up their children in the Christian faith?

Families can give children their first experiences of love, loyalty, forgiveness and tolerance.

Families can take care of the sick and the elderly.

Family members can support each other through difficult times, and celebrate good times together.

KEY FACT

Some Christians spend time and money supporting organisations which promote family life.

B Biblical teaching about family life

1 One of the Ten commandments is:

'Honour your father and mother.'   Children should treat their parents with respect and care for them when they are old.

2 The Bible teaches that families have a duty to care for each other:

If anyone does not provide for his relatives, and especially for his immediate family, he has denied the faith and is worse than an unbeliever. (1 Timothy 5:8)

B

3 Children should be respectful to their parents, and parents shouldn't be too hard on their children, but at the same time they should make them well-disciplined:

> Children, obey your parents in everything, for this pleases the Lord.

> Fathers, do not embitter your children, or they will become discouraged. (Colossians 3: 20-21)

Q Do you think Biblical teaching about children and parents is relevant today?

C   The Mothers' Union

The Mothers' Union is a Christian organisation which aims to support family life.

KEY FACT

Remember
You may have learned about the family for subjects such as sociology, but here you are meant to concentrate on religious ideas.

Q What sort of help do you think modern families might need?

- by providing creches and babysitting for single parents
- by supporting the families of people in prison
- by providing counselling and support groups
- by praying for families

It works in all sorts of ways to help families in trouble:

1 Describe Christian teaching about the importance of the family.

2 'Christian parents should always try to make their children follow the Christian faith.' Do you agree? Give reasons to support your answer, and show you have thought about different points of view.

3 Explain why Christians might support the work of an organisation which aims to promote family life.

> If you are asked in your exam about the family, remember there are many different types, and you may wish to mention some of them.

THE BARE BONES

➤ Christians have differing ideas about how men and women should behave, and the roles they should have in Christian life.

➤ The Church of England became sharply divided when people were discussing whether women should be ordained as priests.

A Women in society

KEY FACT

The society Jesus lived in was patriarchal (men were in charge). Some Christians believe society today should still be like this, with men taking the lead and women supporting them and caring for children. Other Christians think this is an old-fashioned view and inappropriate for the modern world.

Remember
In general, the Bible seems to favour the view that women should take a secondary role – but the Bible was written a very long time ago, and some Christians think that this should change.

• Some Christians believe men and women should have **equality** in society. The Bible teaches that people should forget their differences once they become Christians:

> There is neither Jew nor Greek, slave nor free, male nor female, for you are all one in Christ Jesus. (Galatians 3:28).

INTERNATIONAL WOMEN'S DAY

• They believe women should be able to work outside the home if they want to, and they should expect their partners to share the housework and childcare.

• Some Christians believe men are meant to be the leaders, and women should support their husbands rather than try to be equal. They believe men and women have **different skills**, and women should take on the role of carer. The Bible teaches:

> For the husband is the head of the wife as Christ is the head of the church, his body, of which he is the Saviour. Now as the church submits to Christ, so also wives should submit to their husbands in everything. (Ephesians 5:22-24)

Q In what ways do Christian churches show respect for women?

B Women in church

The Roman Catholic and Orthodox Churches believe women should not be ordained as priests.

They believe this because:

- When the priest celebrates the Eucharist (Mass), he represents Christ making his sacrifice. It would be inappropriate for a woman to do this.

- Jesus chose men, not women, to be his apostles. Women have many skills, but Christian leadership is not one of them.

- The Bible teaches that women should not preach in church, and Christians should follow what the Bible says.

Other churches such as the Methodists, the United Reformed Church and, since 1994, the Church of England, do ordain women as priests.

They do this because:

- They believe if a person is right for the job of leading a church, it should not matter whether they are male or female.

- The think the Church should set an example to the rest of the world by encouraging equality.

- They say Jesus lived in a very different sort of society from the one we have today, and it would be wrong today to treat women in the way they used to be treated in the first century.

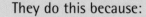

Q What are the main arguments for and against the ordination of women?

1 Explain Christian teaching which might be used in a discussion about equality between men and women.

2 'A Christian wife has a duty to support her husband and do what he says.' Do you agree? Give reasons to support your answer and show you have thought about different points of view.

3 Explain why Christians might have different opinions about whether women should be priests.

When discussing the ordination of women, try to cover all the arguments, for and against.

Marriage and divorce

THE BARE BONES

➤ Christians believe marriage is a gift from God.
➤ Christians who marry are expected to treat one another with love and respect, and to remain married for life, until one partner dies.
➤ None of the Christian churches encourage divorce.

A Christian teaching about marriage

KEY FACT

Marriage is becoming less popular as more couples choose to live together without being married. Christians think marriage is still important as a way of showing lifelong commitment in a relationship blessed by God.

- According to the Bible, God always intended men and women be partners for each other, ever since Adam and Eve were first created.
- Christian churches teach that marriage is a gift from God – some, such as the Roman Catholic Church, see marriage as a sacrament, a sacred symbol of the relationship between God and humanity, which can never be undone.
- Christians often believe marriage to be the only proper context for sexual relationships.

Q Why might Christians choose to get married, rather than just live together?

B A Christian wedding

1 Christians who are planning to get married often talk to a priest or minister first, to learn about the things they will promise to each other and what these commitments will mean in practice.

2 They make promises (vows) to each other, saying they will love each other and stay faithful to each other all their lives, whether they are rich or poor, healthy or unhealthy. They make these vows in front of a congregation and before God.

3 The couple often exchange rings as a sign of everlasting love.

4 Prayers are said for the couple, asking God to bless them and to give them children.

C Church teaching about divorce

The Roman Catholic Church teaches that divorce is always wrong, because of Jesus' teaching in Matthew's gospel, which states a man should not divorce his wife, because she will be committing adultery if she remarries. Therefore the Catholic church will not recognise divorce. Married couples who no longer love each other are allowed to live apart, but may not start new sexual relationships with other people. The Church won't allow the re-marriage of divorced people to new partners, because it does not count the divorce as having happened.

The Church of England and other Christian denominations recognise that divorce does happen, although it does not encourage it. Divorced people are allowed to remarry, because of Jesus' teaching about forgiveness.

Q Do you think Christian ideas about marriage and divorce are still appropriate in the modern world?

D The work of Relate

Relate is an example of an organisation Christians might choose to support – even though it is not connected with any religion - because it can help to hold marriages together.

- It aims to help people in their relationships by providing confidential counselling. People can talk through their problems and try to find a way of solving them.

- Relate aims to help people in all kinds of relationships; they do not have to be married or heterosexual.

KEY FACT

Remember
Marriage is important to all Christians, but they have different views about whether divorce is acceptable.

1 'It is wrong to promise to love someone for ever, because you never know how you will feel in years to come.' Do you agree? Give reasons to support your answer, and show you have thought about different points of view. You must refer to Christianity in your answer.

2 Describe Christian teaching about the importance of marriage.

3 Explain why Christians might have different views about whether divorce can ever be right.

If you are asked a question about divorce, try to cover the views of the Catholic Church and other Christian denominations.

The environment

THE BARE BONES

➤ Christians believe the world is God's creation, and continues to belong to God. They believe they have a special responsibility to care for the planet.

➤ The environment today faces many serious problems which threaten the existence of different species.

A Problems facing the environment

KEY FACT

Scientists believe the Earth is facing serious problems because of human behaviour.

Problems such as:

Q What do you think are the most serious environmental problems facing the world?

- **Global warming** – this is an increase in the Earth's temperature, causing climate changes.
- **Deforestation** – this is the destruction of the rainforests and the things that live there.
- **Pollution** – this is caused by dumping waste materials and poisons rather than disposing of them safely.
- **Depletion of natural resources** – this is when things that can't be replaced, like coal and oil, are used up so there is nothing left for the next generation.

KEY FACT

Some people think that because Christians consider humanity to be superior to other forms of life, they are partly responsible for the problems facing the environment today.

B Christian stewardship

KEY FACT

Christians believe they have a responsibility, as 'stewards' to take care of the world God has made.

Remember
The problems facing the environment affect everybody, but Christians they have a duty to thing

Christians believe God made the world at the beginning of time. God put people in charge of the planet, and told them they were to be stewards of the Earth. Stewards take care of things and are responsible when things go wrong; so Christians have a duty to care for the planet, and to try and put things right where they have gone wrong in the past.

C How Christians can help the planet

1 Christians could try to **be less wasteful** with food and fuel.

2 They could use **'greener' types of energy.**

3 They could **recycle things** like glass, paper and aluminium.

4 They could try to **reduce the number of cars** on the road, by sharing vehicles, using public transport or walking and cycling.

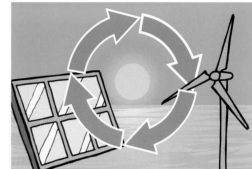

5 They could **use their votes** to support parliamentary candidates who are interested in helping the environment.

6 They could **join an organisation** such as Greenpeace or the Worldwide Fund for Nature.

7 They could **pray** for the future of the planet.

Q Why should Christians care what happens to the planet after their deaths?

1 Explain how Christians might put their beliefs about stewardship of the environment into practice.

2 Explain why Christians might choose to support the work of an organisation which campaigns to protect the environment.

3 'Caring for the environment is the most important thing a Christian can do.' Do you agree? Give reasons to support your answer, and show you have thought about different points of view.

You might know a lot about the environment from other subjects, such as geography, but remember you should concentrate here on religious ideas.

Science and religion

➤ Some people think the theories of science, especially the ideas about how the world began, prove the Bible isn't true.

➤ Other people think that Bible is true and scientists must be wrong.

➤ Other people think scientists and the Bible could both be right, but in different ways.

A Scientific theories vs biblical ideas

KEY FACT

Most scientists believe the universe started with the Big Bang, a massive explosion.

- Scientists also usually believe people did not exist on the Earth at the beginning, but **evolved gradually** over thousands of years, through a process known as **natural selection**. Weaker animals died out, and only the stronger ones survived to reproduce. This idea was first made popular by a man called Charles Darwin in the nineteenth century.

- The Bible teaches that **God made the world in six days**, and then rested on the seventh. It says all plants and animals were made as they appear to us , and doesn't mention evolution. It says everything God made was very good – it doesn't say anything about badly designed animals and plants dying out.

Q Is it possible for someone to be a scientist and a Christian at the same time?

- The Bible teaches that God made people at the beginning of time and not ape-like creatures which later developed into humans. The first people, according to the Bible, were called **Adam and Eve**, and the whole of humanity is descended from this couple.

B Creationists

KEY FACT

Creationists are Christians who believe the world was created exactly as described in Genesis.

- They say **the Bible comes from God, and God doesn't tell lies or make mistakes**. So if the Bible says the world began exactly as described in Genesis, then it did. The scientists must be wrong. Perhaps scientific evidence, such as fossils of animals now extinct, was put there by the Devil to try and trick people into disbelieving the Bible.

Q How do creationists justify their views?

c The biblical story: creation or myth?

Remember
Some Christians believe the world was created by God exactly as described in Genesis, but other Christians think Bible stories could be myths.

Some people say the Genesis story is basically a myth although they believe it is true in some ways. To them God did make the universe, and he did plan everything, making people for a special reason whilst controlling creation. They accept the story might not be literally true in every detail and the universe could have been created gradually, rather than in six days. They suspect the Genesis story is symbolic, rather than historical.

Other people disagree with this view. They might say it's wrong to judge parts of the Bible and say whether or not they are true – we don't know better than the Bible. Or they might disagree because they don't believe in God at all. They might say that using God to explain the existence of the universe is just a lazy way of doing things.

1 'If science is true, Christianity must be wrong.' Do you agree? Give reasons to support your answer, and show you have thought about different points of view.

2 Explain why Christians might have different views about how the world began.

Make sure you have a clear understanding of the differences between scientific and biblical ideas.

Religion and media

THE BARE BONES

➤ Christians use the media in order to publicise the Christian message, and to tell people about organisations and special events.

➤ Sometimes, Christians worry about the influence the media has on society.

A What kinds of media do Christians use?

Posters to tell people about clubs, fund-raising and special events.

Easter Sunday Service 8 pm

Internet for discussion and to teach people about their beliefs.

Newspapers to let people know what's going on in their church in case they want to get involved.

Church Today

Christians use all kinds of media.

Television and radio to bring church services into people's homes, and to broadcast Christian points of view in discussions.

Q How did Christians publicise their faith in the first century?

Christians are sometimes concerned the media has a bad influence on people.

- **Advertising can make people discontented.** They feel they haven't got what other people have, and they want more. It might make them spend money they can't really afford. It might make them feel they deserve to have luxury items, when really they could be giving more money to the poor. Sometimes advertising can encourage prejudices, by making it look as though women love cleaning and men are the only ones interested in money matters or cars.

- **Television and radio dramas can give the impression that it's normal to be involved in crime and violence.** They can give the impression that all married people have affairs and that all teenagers take drugs and get pregnant. The dramas can give the impression that it doesn't matter if everyone copies the main characters in the dramas.

- **Newspapers can sometimes intrude into people's private lives and cause unhappiness, just to make sales.**

- **Internet access can lead people into areas like pornography,** which Christians often think is not healthy.

Q Do you think parents should control what their children watch and read?

C Christians and media censorship

Most Christians recognise the media plays an important role in society.

Some Christians think there should be stricter controls about what is published, so there isn't too much sex and violence on television, and so people are encouraged to live good lives rather than copy bad examples.

Others think adults should be allowed to make their own choices about what they watch and read and listen to, and that they shouldn't need anyone else to interfere.

Q Do you think advertising should be controlled or do you think advertisers should be free to do what they like?

1 Explain why Christians might think the media has advantages and disadvantages.

2 'Television is a bad influence and Christians should not watch it.' Do you agree? Give reasons to support your answer, and show you have thought about different points of view.

Try to give examples of specific programmes, films, newspaper articles or advertisements in your answers.

Exam questions and model answers

Central beliefs

1 a) What happened at the crucifixion of Jesus? (8)

Christians believe on Good Friday, after his trial, Jesus was taken to be crucified. He was nailed to a cross by his hands and feet and left to die. The cross was placed between two criminals. He was given vinegar in a sponge to drink by a Roman soldier. After three hours, he prayed to God, and then he died. A Roman solider pushed a spear into Jesus' side to make sure that he was dead. His mother Mary and John the disciple were with him when he died.

> *This is a straightforward answer which gives a clear account of the crucifixion containing all the important details. In a question like this, there is no need to go beyond the actual events of the crucifixion. The opening sentence helps to put the answer into context.*

b) Explain what happened immediately after Jesus' death. (7)

A rich man called Joseph of Arimathea asked the Roman authorities for Jesus' body. The body was taken down from the cross and placed in a newly-made tomb which belonged to Joseph. A stone was rolled over the entrance to the tomb to cover it. Because it was almost time for the Jewish Sabbath to begin, the body was then left until Sunday.

> *The question asks for an 'explanation' of what happened 'immediately' after Jesus' death. The answer explains what happened and why, e.g. 'because it was almost time for the Jewish Sabbath'. There is no need to go beyond this to the resurrection.*

c) 'It is impossible for Christians in the twenty-first century to follow the example of Jesus.' Do you agree? Give reasons to support your answer and show you have thought about different points of view. (5)

Some people might think that it is impossible to follow the example of Jesus because of all the pressures they are under in modern life. They may feel that they have to work so hard to support their family that they do not have the time to pray and go to church or even to think about helping other people. Others would argue that following the example of Jesus is the most important thing that a Christian can do and that following his example and caring for other people should take priority over everything else.

> *This is a good response taking two viewpoints and supporting them well. It would also have been possible to approach this question by arguing that even if it is impossible to follow Jesus' example, Christians must try to do so.*

d) Describe how and explain why Christians might show respect for the Bible in their daily lives. (7)

The Bible is not treated in the same way as the holy books of some other religions but it is shown respect by Christians. The Bible is believed to be the revealed word of God and is, therefore, very important. Christians will keep a Bible clean and safe and not treat it like any other book. Some Christians read the Bible every day so that they can learn more about God's teachings. In a church, there is often a very large Bible from which people read during the service. In some churches, this is shown great respect and is carried in a procession before it is read. Some people may stand when readings are taken from the gospels. Other Christians show their respect for the Bible simply by trying to follow its teachings in their daily lives.

This is a good answer. It explains the importance of the Bible as well as showing how this importance may be reflected in the way the Bible and its teachings are used.

e) 'Christians should pay more attention to the New Testament than to the Old Testament.'
   Do you agree? Give reasons to support your answer and show you have thought about different points of view. (5)

The whole Bible is important to Christians and is believed to be the revealed word of God, so it is a guide to what God wants and how people should lead their lives. The Old Testament is the Bible of the Jews and shows how God led the Jews to be a chosen people and how they learnt from God's teachings. The New Testament is felt to be more important by some Christians because it contains the accounts of Jesus' life, his teachings and the teachings of the early church.

The answer accepts that the New Testament may be seen as more important because it contains the teachings of Jesus, but also acknowledges a different view about the importance of the Old Testament.

History and Christian life

2 a) Explain why the three main Christian groups are called 'Roman Catholic', 'Orthodox' and 'Protestant'. (7)

At first, the Christian Church was based in Rome and Byzantium (Constantinople). In 1054 CE there was a split between the churches in Rome and Byzantium over differences in teaching. These two groups became the Roman Catholic Church based in Rome with the Pope as its head and the Orthodox Church based in Byzantium under the Patriarch of Constantinople. In the 14th and 15th centuries, some theologians in Europe began to question the power of the Pope and some of the doctrines of the church, in particular the selling of indulgences which were believed to shorten the time people spent in Purgatory. In 1517 Martin Luther nailed a document called the '95 Theses' to the door of his church in Wittenberg. These made allegations against the Catholic Church. This led to the formation of the Protestant churches who were protesting against the Roman Catholic Church.

In a question like this, with limited time to answer, it is important to get the key facts down on paper. This answer picks the main points for the three denominations and expresses them clearly.

b) 'Each Christian group should be proud of the teachings and practices which make it special and different.'
Do you agree? Give reasons to support your answer and show that you have thought about different points of view. (5)

Each of the Christian churches is different. They all have particular practices which are important to them. The Orthodox Church is one of the oldest and is very proud of its traditions and the way in which it worships. The Roman Catholic Church is the largest Christian group. However, although people think that their particular practices and beliefs are very important, they are all Christians who follow the example of the life and teachings of Jesus and they all believe that Jesus was the Son of God who gave his life to save humanity from sin. Therefore, some people believe that the churches should forget their differences and come together in one group.

> *This is a good response which clearly shows two sides to the discussion.*

c) Describe the main features of a Christian place of worship. (8)

The buildings used by Christians for worship are often quite different from each other. However, many have the same main features. The font is one of the most important features because it's where babies are baptised and welcomed into the Christian church. The font is usually found near the main door of the church. The altar is also very important. It usually stands towards the east end of the church, though sometimes it is right in the centre. The Eucharist is celebrated on the altar. Another very important feature is the pulpit. This is a raised platform where the priest or minister may stand to give the sermon. It is high up so that everyone can hear. Sometimes the pulpit is also used for bible readings. In some churches, the bible is read from a stand called a lectern.

> *The question asks for the 'main' features. The answer focuses on three features which are all important in regard to Christian faith and worship. The opening sentence shows that the candidate is aware that not all churches and their features are the same.*

d) Describe one example of ecumenism in Christianity. (8)

One example of ecumenism is the World Council of Churches. This was founded after the Second World War in 1948 by Christians who wanted to do something about restoring peace in the world. Many Christians believe it is important to work together, because disagreements and divisions give a bad impression of the Christian message of love, and prevent important aims, such as caring for the poor. The World Council of Churches was set up to promote Christian unity, to act as a voice in the world, and to help bring about peace and justice in accordance with Christian principles. Christian Aid is the overseas aid agency for the World Council of Churches.

> *There are many examples which could have been chosen here such as the work of an ecumenical centre, but the World Council of Churches is a good example and the answer explains its purpose clearly.*

3 a) Explain the meaning and importance of baptism for Christians. (7)

Baptism is a sacrament – the outward visible sign of an inward invisible grace. It is important for Christians because the baby is blessed and is now free from Original Sin. It has become a member of the Christian Church. Some other Christians, such as Baptists, believe that baptism should wait until the person is old enough to make the decision for themselves. In the Baptist church, people choose to be baptised as adults and this takes place by total immersion in a large pool at the front of the church.

> *The question asks for an explanation and the answer provides a good account of the purpose of Baptism, in cleansing Original Sin, as well as the welcoming of the baby into the Christian Church.*

b) Describe what is said and done at an infant baptism. (8)

At an infant baptism the baby is brought to church by its parents. The priest, the parents and the godparents stand by the font. The priest holds the baby and asks the godparents to make promises on its behalf. They promise that they will bring the baby up to be a Christian. The priest then makes the sign off the cross with water on the baby's forehead and blesses the baby in the 'Name of the Father, the Son and the Holy Spirit'. Sometimes each person at the ceremony carries a candle because Jesus brought light into the world.

> *The question does not ask for a baptism in any particular denomination and the answer is therefore a general description of the ceremony. All the main details are included, in particular the use of the Triune name: 'Father, Son and Holy Spirit'.*

c) Describe what is said and done at a Christian funeral. (8)

At a Christian funeral the body is usually taken into a church in a coffin. It is placed at the front of the church while a priest or minister conducts a short service. Someone will say something about the life of the person who has died. Prayers are said asking God to take care of the person in the hope that they have now gone to heaven. The person leading the service reminds the congregation that Jesus said, 'I am the resurrection and the life'. After the service, the body may be taken to a graveyard to be buried or to a crematorium to be cremated. The words, 'ashes to ashes, dust to dust' are said to remind people that their bodies return to the earth but their souls go to heaven.

> *This is a good account of a typical Christian funeral containing all the important details. The quotation is useful because it shows an understanding of this particularly Christian teaching about death.*

d) 'Easter is the most important Christian festival.'
   Do you agree? Give reasons to support your answer and show you have thought about different points of view. (5)

Easter recalls the time when Jesus overcame death. On the Sunday morning, when the women visited the tomb they found that it was empty and Jesus was alive again. This means that all followers of Jesus now had the opportunity to receive eternal life and need not fear death. Because of this, Easter is the most important Christian festival. However, some people believe that Christmas is particularly important because this was the moment when God chose to become man and live on earth as Jesus. This is called the Incarnation.

> *The answer is well-balanced, it shows two points of view about the statement and each is well-supported with argument.*

e) Explain how beliefs about the afterlife might affect the way Christians live. (7)

Christians believe if they follow the example of Jesus and his teachings and accept him as the Son of God they will go to heaven when they die. They may also believe if they do not do this they will go to hell. Therefore, they may make sure throughout their life that they always try to act in the way Jesus taught, in particular they may follow his teaching of 'agape' or Christian love.

> *The answer shows the essential Christian beliefs about life after death. It would also have been possible to mention Purgatory here. It shows that Christians must believe in Jesus as well as follow his teachings.*

Wealth and poverty

4 a) Describe the work of a Christian organisation which helps the poor in developing countries. (8)

The organisation I have chosen is Christian Aid. Christian Aid works in a number of different ways. It raises funds throughout the year, but especially during Christian Aid week in May. Some of the money is spent on emergency relief, such as providing food, shelter and medicine in times of famine or war. Other money is spent on long-term projects. Christian Aid tries not to send too many workers overseas. It treats people in developing countries as partners, and allows them to make decisions about what is needed and how the money should be used. Christian Aid gives money to people in need whether they are Christian or not. It supports health education, immunisation, literacy programmes, teaching people new skills, and helps people to provide their communities with clean water. It also provides education for people in the UK so that they can learn more about how their behaviour affects developing countries.

> *This answer scores full marks because the candidate has chosen an organisation which is explicitly Christian, concentrating on describing its work, rather than its history or Biblical teaching. The writer shows that he or she knows about this organisation, and is able to give specific examples rather than just saying vaguely that they give food to people who are hungry.*

b) Explain why a Christian might believe it is important to support overseas aid agencies. (7)

Christians believe they have a duty to help the poor, because this is taught all the way through the Bible, in Leviticus, Amos, the Sermon on the Mount, the parable of the Sheep and the Goats, and other places too. The Bible teaches 'always treat others as you would like to be treated yourself'. Christians think about how they would like to be treated if they were poor, and they try to do this for others. Even if the poor people live in another country, Christians should still treat them as neighbours and care for them. They can't give food to people who are a long way away, so they might support an overseas agency such as Christian Aid, CAFOD or Tearfund, who will know how to use their donations well.

> *This candidate scores full marks again, because he or she has given several different reasons why Christians should help the poor, and is able to back them up. The writer might be running out of time by now, so the Bible teachings are not detailed, but it is still clear that he or she knows them because a good selection has been made.*

c) 'Caring for the poor is the most important part of being a Christian.'
   Do you agree? Give reasons to support your answer, and show you have thought about different points of view. (5)

I disagree, because I think that going to church on Sunday is the most important part of being a Christian. Lots of people give to the poor, whether they are Christian or not, but going to church shows your belief in God. Up to a point, I think the statement is true, because if there are poor people around you and you don't do anything to help them, then you aren't loving God and loving your neighbour. Some people, like Mother Teresa, would agree with the statement.

> *This gets full marks, because the candidate has given his or her own point of view with a reason. The writer also discusses Christian teaching on the subject, and shows he or she recognises other people might have different views.*

Medical ethics

5 a) Explain Christian teachings that might be used in a discussion about euthanasia. (8)

Euthanasia means 'a good death'. It means bringing someone's life to an end more quickly, often because the person is in a lot of pain or is severely disabled. Euthanasia is sometimes called 'assisted suicide', because it is intended for people who are unable to take their own lives without help.

The Bible says nothing about euthanasia because it was written before euthanasia was a medical issue. However, it does teach 'Do not kill' in the Ten Commandments. It teaches that all humans are made 'in the image of God'. These teachings might be used to show euthanasia is wrong. Some Christians believe the commandment 'always treat others as you would like to be treated' shows euthanasia can sometimes be right, if it is what you would want for yourself in that situation. The churches believe euthanasia to be wrong, but they do say life does not have to be kept going at all costs.

This would score full marks. The answer shows an understanding of what euthanasia means, but the answer does not concentrate too heavily on scientific detail or on listing different forms of euthanasia, because the specifically question asked about Christian teaching. Several examples of Biblical teaching are given as well as different Christian views about euthanasia. The candidate knows that the churches have made statements about euthanasia and has summarised what they have said.

b) Explain how and why Christians might support the work of an organisation which tries to prevent suicide. (7)

Christians believe suicide is wrong, but they also accept people only try to commit suicide when they are desperate and feel they have no other choice. They believe human life is a gift from God, and it is sacred because God made people 'in his own image' (Genesis 1:26). One of the commandments is 'Do not commit murder' and some people think suicide is similar to murder even if the victim and the murderer are the same person. They think suicide shows ungratefulness for the gift of life and unwillingness to accept suffering. Christians believe people who are tempted to commit suicide need help and loving support, not judgement.

One organisation they might support is the Samaritans. This organisation uses volunteers to talk to people who are thinking of committing suicide, to let them know someone cares about them. Christians might volunteer to become Samaritans, or they might take part in fund-raising for it, or they might help to advertise its work so more people know where they can turn if they feel suicidal.

This answer would score full marks. It shows understanding of why Christians would want to help prevent suicides, as well as what they might do. The answer gives some Biblical examples to illustrate the main points. The candidate knows of an organisation which helps people who are thinking of committing suicide, and is able to give some practical examples to show how Christian belief might make someone behave in a particular way.

c) 'Human life should be preserved in all circumstances.' Do you agree? Give reasons to support your answer and show you have thought about different points of view. You must refer to Christianity in your answer. (5)

Some Christians think all human life should be preserved, whether it is a foetus before birth, a baby born with serious abnormalities, or someone in a lot of pain with a terminal illness. They believe only God should decide when someone dies, and they think human life is sacred. Other Christians believe it is sometimes better not to preserve the life. For example, if a foetus had serious problems, it might be better to end the pregnancy with abortion. If someone was dying in pain, and had a heart attack, it might be better not to resuscitate them. They might think it is more important to do the most loving thing, rather than preserve the life.

My own view is that people should be allowed to end life when it seems the right choice for them. I don't believe in God, and I think humans have the right to decide whether to have abortions or euthanasia, because I would want to have these choices available to me in some circumstances.

War, peace and justice

6 a) Describe Biblical teaching which might be used to support the view that it is never right to fight in a war. (8)

Some parts of the Bible seem to support the idea that fighting in a war can sometimes be right. But there are also Biblical passages which say that Christians should live in peace. The prophet Isaiah said the Messiah would be the 'Prince of Peace', and Christians believe Jesus was the Messiah, coming to bring peace into the world. Jesus said that the peace-makers would be blessed, and he told people they should love their enemies and pray for them. Christians might feel it is impossible to love your enemy if you are dropping bombs on him or her at the same time.

The Bible teaches you should love God and your neighbour, and you should treat everyone as your neighbour, which would include enemies. It says you should treat other people as you would like to be treated yourself, which could mean not fighting with them.

b) Describe how and explain why Christians might work to support the victims of abuses of human rights. (7)

Christians believe that everyone is valuable to God. It doesn't matter how old they are, or what race they are, or whether they are men or women. The parable of the Sheep and the Goats says that whatever people do for each other, they do for God. Christians believe you should treat others in the way you would like to be treated, so they think about how they would feel if their human rights were abused.

Some Christians have worked for the victims of human rights abuses by following the teaching of Liberation Theology, and fighting for the poor and the oppressed, even if it means risking their own lives. Camilo Torres and Oscar Romero are examples of Christians who did this. Other Christians might support an organisation such as Amnesty International, which runs campaigns to help people who are being tortured or imprisoned because of their beliefs. Christians might support this by fund-raising, writing letters to governments and communicating with people in prison.

This is a good answer because the candidate shows how Christian beliefs might be put into practice. The Christian belief in human rights is explained, and this is backed up with examples of Christian teaching. The writer shows a knowledge of Liberation Theology and of Amnesty International, but notices that he or she was not asked to give a lot of historical background. Instead, examples are given of what Christians might do.

c) 'It is cowardly to be a pacifist.' Do you agree? Give reasons to support your answer, and show you have thought about different points of view. You must refer to Christianity in your answer. (5)

Some Christians think fighting for your country in war-time is right, because it defends the weak. They think if an enemy is doing something wrong, such as killing the Jews, then it is cowardly to sit back and do nothing. People should be prepared to risk their lives to help others, by fighting. Other Christians, such as Quakers, believe it is never right to fight or use violence, because Christians are taught to love their enemies.

I think sometimes people refuse to fight because they are cowards. But sometimes, it can take a lot of bravery to be non-violent. Martin Luther King refused to use violence, but he still risked his own life for Civil Rights, and he was shot. When people are conscientious objectors, they are often given dangerous jobs such as driving ambulances through fierce fighting, and this takes a lot of bravery. So I think the statement can be true in some cases, but not always.

Here, the candidate gains full marks because different points of view have been considered. He or she has included Christian thinking in the answer, and shown an understanding of why people might feel differently about this issue. The writer has backed up the different arguments with reasons, and explained his or her own view.

Family, relationships and gender

7 a) Explain Christian teaching about the importance of the family. (8)

The book of Genesis teaches that the reason God made men and women was so they could get married and have families. The family is important for Christians, because they believe it is one of the best contexts for children to learn about Christian life, and to learn about love and loyalty. Families are often in the best position to give hospitality to people in need. They might be able to adopt or foster other children or look after someone elderly. They can support and protect each other. The Mothers' Union is an example of a Christian organisation which aims to provide support for family life.

The churches teach that traditional families are an important part of a stable society, but Christianity does not teach that all adults should marry and have children. Roman Catholic priests are not allowed to marry, and monks and nuns are very much respected by Christians.

This answer would gain full marks because it shows an understanding of the different ways in which the family is important in Christianity. It refers to Biblical teaching, and also to the teaching of the churches. It shows an understanding that it is not compulsory in Christianity to marry, but that marriage is valued.

b) 'Marriage is out of date.'
   Do you agree? Give reasons to support your answer and show you have thought about different points of view. You must refer to Christianity in your answer. (5)

Today, many marriages end in divorce and the number is increasing. Also, many people decide that they do not need to get married and so they just live together instead without any formal ceremony. However, Christians believe that marriage is very important and that couples should not live together until they are married. Marriage is a sacrament and a promise made to God that the two people will stay together, look after each other and be faithful to each other. Christians believe that this will provide a stable home for children and one of the main purposes of marriage is so that the couple will have children.

This question gives plenty of scope for discussion. The answer shows a 'modern view' of relationships where people choose to live together while also explaining the importance of marriage for Christians.

c) Explain how a married couple's Christian faith might affect the way they behave towards each other. (7)

If a couple are Christians, they would probably have been married in church and made vows to each other before God. They would have promised to love each other whether they are rich or poor, sick or healthy. They would have promised to be faithful to each other all their lives. Roman Catholics believe marriage is a sacrament, and that it shows the relationship between Christ and the church. Christians believe marriage is for life, so a married Christian couple would try hard to be faithful to each other. If their marriage ran into trouble, they would work hard to put it right, perhaps by using an organisation such as 'Relate'.

Some Christians believe the man should be head of the family, and the wife should submit to him when there are decisions to be made. This might mean he becomes the main earner and she stays at home more and looks after the children and supports him in his career. Others think Christianity teaches that all people are equal, so they might have more of an equal partnership. Christian couples should treat each other with respect, honesty and love.

This answer would gain full marks because the candidate includes several different ideas, all relevant to the question. The answer concentrates on Christian beliefs, rather than just writing about marriage in general terms. The writer shows that he or she understands these beliefs, and writes about how they might affect the way a married couple interacts.

d) 'In a Christian family, the man should be the leader.'
Do you agree? Give reasons to support your answer, and show you have thought about different points of view. (5)

In the Bible, there are different views about the relation between men and women in married life, so Christians have different views about it. Some Christians believe that the man should be the head of the household, because there is teaching in some of the New Testament letters saying that wives should submit to their husbands. Others believe that all people are equal (Galatians) and that there doesn't need to be one 'leader' in a family, everyone should share decisions.

My own view is that men should take the lead at home, because women are better at housework and childcare, and men earn more money so they should make important decisions at home.

> *This answer would gain full marks, because the candidate has looked at different points of view and referred to Christianity. There's an understanding of why people might have different opinions about this, and the writer's own view is given, backed up with reasons. The writer's view isn't necessarily one that the examiners will share, but this doesn't stop him or her getting the marks. He or she is entitled to his or her opinion, and the marks are for whether the view is relevant and whether the writer can give a reason for it.*

Science, religion and the environment

8 a) Explain Christian beliefs about the origins of the world. (8)

The book of Genesis in the Bible teaches the world was created by God in six days. It teaches that all the different species existed from the beginning of time, and not that they evolved gradually. It says everything that was made was 'very good'. It was all created by God's word – God said 'Let there be... ' and there was. God made the sun, moon and stars as well as the earth. Humans were made to complete creation and to look after it, but Adam and Eve, the first people, were tempted by the serpent to disobey God and eat the fruit of the forbidden tree. Because of this, they were sent out of the Garden of Eden.

Some Christians believe this story is literally true, and everything happened exactly as Genesis describes it. Other Christians believe this story is a myth, a poetic way of telling truth about God and the world, but not necessarily describing real events.

> *This answer gains full marks because the candidate shows that he or she knows in detail about Biblical teaching, with regard to the origins of the world. The answer shows Christians have different views about how this should be interpreted, and doesn't just assume that all Christians take the stories literally.*

b) Describe how and explain why Christians might work to protect the environment. (7)

Christians believe God gave humans the responsibility to be 'stewards of the earth' (Genesis). This means they have a duty to care for it and preserve it. Christians also believe they should show love for other people, including future generations, so they should make sure people who live on the planet in the future have enough resources and a suitable climate.

Christians might work to help the environment by joining an organisation such as Friends of the Earth or the World Wide Fund for Nature, which campaign for environmental issues. They might use their votes to keep people in power who have 'green' policies. They might go on demonstrations. They might recycle bottles and paper and aluminium and clothing, drive cars which use less fuel or use public transport more often, and avoid dropping litter.

> *Here the candidate gains full marks because he or she has noticed the question asks 'describe how...' and then gives lots of examples. The question also asks 'explain why...' so Christian teaching is discussed to show that the writer understands the reasons why Christians believe they should care for the environment.*

c) 'If the Bible is right about how the world was made, the theories of science must be wrong.'

Do you agree? Give reasons to support your answer, and show you have thought about different points of view. You must refer to Christianity in your answer. (5)

The theories of science teach that the universe was made by a Big Bang, and people were formed over a long time through the processes of evolution and natural selection. The Bible, on the other hand, teaches that everything was made in six days, by God. Some people think these different ideas contradict each other completely. Christians might say scientists must be wrong because the Bible comes from God and God does not make mistakes, and scientists might say that the Bible was written before people understood science, and we know better now. Other people think the two ideas can work together, if you don't take the Bible literally but treat it as myth. My own view is that the scientists are right, because their theories are supported with evidence, but the Bible isn't.

> *This would score full marks because the candidate has kept closely to what he or she was asked to do. No time is wasted explaining scientific theories in detail or re-telling the story of Genesis, because the question is asking for evaluation and discussion. The writer gives his or her own view, refers to Christianity and looks at more than one opinion.*

Topic checker

- After you've revised a topic, go through these questions.
- Put a tick if you know the answer, a cross if you don't (you can check your answer at the bottom of each section).
- Try the questions again until you've got a column that are all ticks! Then you'll know you can be confident.

Central beliefs

1 Who are the three 'persons' of the Trinity?	☐	☐	☐
2 What are the two sections of the Bible?	☐	☐	☐
3 Where was Jesus born?	☐	☐	☐
4 Who were Jesus' mother and father?	☐	☐	☐
5 Who was given the Ten Commandments?	☐	☐	☐
6 Name three of the Ten Commandments.	☐	☐	☐
7 Who preached the Sermon on the Mount?	☐	☐	☐
8 What are the Beatitudes?	☐	☐	☐
9 Who was Paul?	☐	☐	☐
10 Explain what is meant by 'the problem of evil'.	☐	☐	☐
11 What does the Book of Job teach about suffering?	☐	☐	☐
12 What is the difference between 'moral evil' and 'natural evil'?	☐	☐	☐

Answers 1 God the Father, God the Son, God the Holy Spirit 2 Old Testament, New Testament 3 Bethlehem 4 Mary and Joseph (earthly father) or God (real father) 5 Moses 6 1 You shall have no other gods 2 You shall not worship idols 3 You shall not misuse the name of God 4 Remember the Sabbath day and keep it holy 5 Honour your father and mother 6 You shall not murder 7 You shall not commit adultery 8 You shall not steal 9 You shall not give false testimony against your neighbour 10 You shall not covet (be envious of) your neighbour's possessions 7 Jesus 8 The first section of the Sermon on the Mount, beginning, 'Blessed are...'

9 A Jew who had a vision that Jesus called him. He began to preach the message of Christianity throughout the Mediterranean. 10 It means the problems raised by the existence of evil and suffering in the world, because this suggests that there cannot be a God who is all-loving and all-powerful (omnipotent). 11 It teaches that suffering should be accepted with patience and faith, and that people should not expect to understand what God chooses to do. 12 Moral evil is the wrong caused by human wickedness, such as murder or violence. Natural evil is suffering caused by nature, such a disease, drought or earthquake.

13 What are the three main divisions of the Church?	☐ ☐ ☐
14 Who is the Pope?	☐ ☐ ☐
15 Why is the Patriarch of Constantinople important?	☐ ☐ ☐
16 Name two non-Conformist churches.	☐ ☐ ☐
17 What does ecumenism mean?	☐ ☐ ☐
18 What is the World Council of Churches?	☐ ☐ ☐
19 What is a font?	☐ ☐ ☐
20 Why is the altar important in many churches?	☐ ☐ ☐
21 What is the pulpit used for?	☐ ☐ ☐
22 What is a pilgrimage?	☐ ☐ ☐
23 Where might Christians go on pilgrimage?	☐ ☐ ☐
24 Name three types of prayer.	☐ ☐ ☐
25 Name two well-known prayers.	☐ ☐ ☐

Answers 13 Orthodox, Roman Catholic, Protestant 14 Head of the Roman Catholic Church 15 He is head of the Orthodox Church 16 There are many you could choose: Baptist, Methodist, and United Reformed are examples 17 Ecumenism is the name given to the belief that all churches should try to become more united. It is a movement that encourages Christians to worship together and forget their differences. 18 The World Council of Churches was formed after the Second World War, in 1948, by Christians who wanted to do something about restoring peace in the world. The WCC promotes ecumenism by encouraging Christians to work more closely together. 19 A bowl that holds the water for baptism 20 Because the Eucharist is celebrated there 21 For preaching and sometimes for reading the Bible 22 A journey to a special place associated with a religion 23 There are many you could choose: Rome, Lourdes, Walsingham, and the Holy Land are examples 24 Petitionary prayer is when people ask God for something, for themselves or for other people. Intercessory prayer is when people ask God to intervene in the world at a time of crisis or when people are starving or suffering because of a disaster. Prayers to give thanks. 25 Lord's Prayer, Hail Mary, Jesus Prayer

Sacraments

26 What happens at a baptism?	☐	☐	☐
27 What is Original Sin?	☐	☐	☐
28 Why do some people get confirmed?	☐	☐	☐
29 What are the vows in a marriage ceremony?	☐	☐	☐
30 What do Christians believe about life after death?	☐	☐	☐
31 What is purgatory?	☐	☐	☐

Holy days

32 What is Advent?	☐	☐	☐
33 Why is Christmas such an important festival for Christians?	☐	☐	☐
34 What does Lent recall?	☐	☐	☐
35 What happened during Holy Week?	☐	☐	☐
36 What happened on Easter Sunday?	☐	☐	☐
37 What was the Ascension?	☐	☐	☐
38 What happened at the first Pentecost?	☐	☐	☐

Answers 26 The sign of the cross is made on the baby's forehead with water and he or she is blessed in the 'Name of the Father, the Son and the Holy Spirit'. 27 Christians believe that, because of the disobedience of Adam and Eve in the garden of Eden, all people are born with Original Sin. This sin needs to be removed before people can truly live their lives as Christians. 28 They choose to make promises to God themselves to live a Christian life. 29 The promises that the couple make to each other and to God. 30 Christians believe that when they die they will have the chance of eternal life. Christians believe that they may go to heaven, hell or purgatory, depending on how well they have lived on earth. 31 Some Christians believe that most people are probably not good enough to go straight to heaven because of sins they have committed on earth, but they have believed in Jesus so they will not go to hell. Instead, they are taken to Purgatory where they are punished for a period of time before they are able to enter heaven. 32 The four weeks of preparation before Christmas. 33 Because it celebrates the incarnation, the birth of Jesus. 34 The forty days that Jesus spent in the wilderness after his baptism. 35 Jesus preached in Jerusalem and ate the Last Supper with his disciples. 36 Jesus rose from the dead. 37 The time when Jesus finally left his disciples and went up to heaven. 38 The disciples received the gift of the Holy Spirit.

Wealth and poverty

39 What did the prophet Amos teach about how people should treat the poor?	☐ ☐ ☐
40 Give three examples of work a Christian aid agency might do in a developing country.	☐ ☐ ☐
41 What is the parable of the rich man and Lazarus about?	☐ ☐ ☐
42 Give three examples of occupations that a Christian might consider to be wrong ways of earning money.	☐ ☐ ☐
43 What is the parable of the Sheep and the Goats about?	☐ ☐ ☐

Medical ethics

44 What is meant by the phrase 'the sanctity of life'?	☐ ☐ ☐
45 Name an organisation Christians might support, which helps people who are thinking of committing suicide.	☐ ☐ ☐
46 What is meant by 'passive euthanasia'?	☐ ☐ ☐
47 Why might some Christians be in favour of euthanasia?	☐ ☐ ☐
48 What do Roman Catholics believe about the use of contraception?	☐ ☐ ☐
49 Give an example of Christian teaching that might be used to support the view that abortion is wrong.	☐ ☐ ☐
50 Give three things a Christian might do to put into practice the belief that abortion is wrong.	☐ ☐ ☐
51 Why might some Christians be in favour of embryo research?	☐ ☐ ☐

Answers 39 He taught that the poor should be treated with justice; he taught that God would punish those who were unkind to the poor. 40 There are many examples you could use including: providing emergency relief such as food, shelter and medicines in times of disaster; providing clean water; giving health education; teaching literacy skills; supporting fair trade; helping people to learn new skills; supporting women's co-operatives. 41 It says that it is wrong to ignore the poor. 42 There are many examples you could choose: jobs that depend on pornography, gambling, drugs, alcohol or tobacco, prostitution, crime, etc. 43 It teaches that whatever people do to care for each other, they are doing it for Jesus, and when they ignore people in need, they ignore Jesus. They will be judged according to how they treat others. 44 It means the holiness of life – it shows the belief that all life is given by God and is special. 45 The Samaritans 46 It means that someone's life ends because treatment that could have helped him or her to live longer is not given, so that death comes more quickly. 47 They might believe that it is the kindest way to help someone in pain. They might try to treat the person in the way that they would like to be treated themselves if they had a painful illness or serious disability. 48 They believe that only natural methods should be used, not artificial. 49 There are many examples you could use: perhaps Psalm 139 (you knew me before I was born), or Exodus 20:13 (do not murder). 50 They might use their vote to support anti-abortion campaigns; go on a march; lobby their MP; join a letter-writing campaign; work for an adoption agency; support an organisation such as Life or SPUC. 51 They might believe that it provides an opportunity for discovering more about curing serious illnesses, and therefore it is a loving thing to do. They might argue that Jesus was a healer. They might say that the embryos used would have been wasted otherwise, and this helps some good to come out of abortion.

52 What does IVF stand for?	☐ ☐ ☐
53 Why might some Christians be against fertility treatment?	☐ ☐ ☐
54 What is Dame Cicely Saunders famous for?	☐ ☐ ☐

War, peace and justice

55 What opinion would you expect a Quaker (a member of the Religious Society of Friends) to have about whether it is right to fight in a war?	☐ ☐ ☐
56 What is a 'conscientious objector'?	☐ ☐ ☐
57 Who set down the conditions necessary for a Just War?	☐ ☐ ☐
58 Name an organisation Christians might support, which helps the victims of human rights abuses.	☐ ☐ ☐
59 In which book of the Bible does it say that people were created in the image of God?	☐ ☐ ☐
60 Why might some Christians be in favour of capital punishment?	☐ ☐ ☐
61 Which parable told by Jesus illustrates the point that everyone should be treated as a neighbour, whatever their race?	☐ ☐ ☐
62 What was Martin Luther King's 'I have a dream' speech about?	☐ ☐ ☐
63 What was apartheid?	☐ ☐ ☐
64 What is Trevor Huddleston famous for?	☐ ☐ ☐

Answers 52 In Vitro Fertilisation (fertilisation in glass). 53 They might believe that it interferes with God's plans for that couple. They might be worried about it being used for people who would not naturally have children, such as homosexual couples or women beyond the natural age for childbirth. They might worry about what happens to spare embryos. They might be concerned that AID introduces a third adult into a married relationship. 54 She promoted the modern hospice movement in the UK, to provide care for the dying. 55 They are likely to be pacifists and choose not to fight. 56 It is someone who objects to fighting in a war because his or her conscience says that war is wrong. 57 Thomas Aquinas 58 Amnesty International 59 Genesis 60 They might believe that it shows justice. Capital punishment is recommended in the Bible for some crimes. They might think it is kinder to the victim and their family to prevent the criminal from ever repeating the crime. They might think it is more humane than a life sentence. 61 The Parable of the Good Samaritan 62 It was about his dream for the future, when black and white people would live together peacefully and equally. 63 It was a system in South Africa which made it illegal for black and white people to mix. It gave many rights and privileges to white people, and very few to black people. 64 He was a Christian priest who fought against apartheid.

Family, relationships and gender

65 What do Roman Catholics believe about divorce?	☐	☐	☐
66 What does the Church of England teach about divorce?	☐	☐	☐
67 What Biblical teaching might a Christian use to support the view that men should have a leadership role in the home and in church?	☐	☐	☐

Global issues

68 In which book of the Bible does it say that people are to be the stewards of the earth?	☐	☐	☐
69 Name an organisation that a Christian might choose to support, which aims to help conserve and protect the environment.	☐	☐	☐
70 Give three ways in which a Christian might show concern for the environment.	☐	☐	☐
71 Why might some Christians disagree with scientific theories about the way the world began?	☐	☐	☐
72 Name a scientist famous for developing the theory of evolution and the theory of natural selection.	☐	☐	☐

Answers 65 They believe that marriage is a sacrament for life, and so they do not recognise divorce.
66 It teaches that ideally marriage should be for life, but it recognises divorce. Divorced people can be remarried in church as long as the vicar agrees.
67 Possibly 1 Timothy 2:9-12 (wives behave modestly and submit to your husbands), or Titus 2:5 (wives be busy at home and submit to your husbands).
68 Genesis 69 There are many you could choose: Greenpeace, the World Wide Fund for Nature, Friends of the Earth are examples. 70 There are many examples you could choose, including: recycling, using less packaging, using public transport, economising on fuel, lobbying MPs on environmental issues, joining a conservation group. 71 They might believe that the Biblical account of creation, given in Genesis, is literally true, and it does not match scientific theories.
72 Charles Darwin; Alfred Wallace

Complete the facts

Festivals

1   Join the festival to the event it commemorates.

Name of festival	Event it commemorates
Advent	Last week in Jesus' life
Christmas	Jesus returns to heaven
Lent	Birth of Jesus
Holy Week	Holy Spirit comes to the disciples
Good Friday	Jesus' resurrection
Easter Sunday	Preparing for Jesus' birth
Ascension	Jesus' crucifixion
Pentecost	Jesus' temptation in the wilderness

Church features

2   Fill in the following table.

Feature	What is this for?
Altar	
Pulpit	
Spire or tower	
Pool in a Baptist church	

Organisations Christians might support

3   Complete the following table.

Organisation	What it does	Is it explicitly Christian? (Y/N)
Amnesty International		
The Mothers' Union		
Greenpeace		
CAFOD		
Relate		
Save the Children		

Rites of passage

4   In the left-hand column is a list of items and people that can be linked to the
    Christian rites of passage of baptism, confirmation, marriage and funerals. Tick the
    correct box(es) for each item or person.

ITEM/PERSON	Baptism	Confirmation	Marriage	Funerals
Altar				
Font				
Ring				
Sacrament				
Bishop				
Water				
Godparents				
Oil				
Nuptial mass				
Priest				
Cremation				
Vows				

Medical ethics

5   Use the words below to complete the following sentences about medical ethics.

wrong	acceptable	anctity	voluntary
abortion	embryos	fertility treatment	Saunders

* When a pregnancy ends before the baby is ready to be born, this is called an
  ....

* There are different kinds of euthanasia. When someone makes a deliberate choice
  to have his or her life ended, this is called assisted suicide or ....
  euthanasia.

* IVF, AID and AIH are all forms of ....

* The Roman Catholic church teaches that abortion is always ....

* .... of life is another way of saying that life is holy and sacred.

* Dame Cicely .... was famous for her work in the hospice movement.

* The Church of England and the Methodist church teach that using contraception is
  ....

* Scientists are trying to find cures for Motor Neurone Disease and Parkinson's
  Disease by performing research on spare .... produced during abortions.

Care for the poor

6 Complete the following Biblical quotations about care for the poor.

a) Blessed are you who are poor, for yours is.... (Luke 6:20)

_____

b) On the first day of every week, each of you is to put aside and ...
(1 Corinthians 16:2)

_____

c) He looked up and saw rich people putting their gifts into the treasury; he also saw a poor widow put in two small copper coins. He said, "Truly I tell you, this poor widow has put in more than all of them; for all of the have contributed out of their abundance, but she out of her poverty has put in..." (Luke 21:1-4)

_____

d) No one can serve two masters; for a slave will either..., or be devoted to the one and despise the other. You cannot serve God and wealth. (Matthew 6:24)

_____

e) The love of money is the... (1 Timothy 6:10)

_____

f) You lack one thing: go, sell what you own, and..., and you will have treasure in heaven; then come, follow me." When he heard this, he was shocked and went away grieving, for he had many possessions. (Mark 10:21-22)

_____

Racial prejudice

7 True or false? Mark with a T or F in the box your answer to the following questions.

a) Jesus told the parable of the Good Samaritan to answer the question: 'What must I do to be saved?' ☐

b) The quotation 'Do not ill-treat foreigners who are living in your land' comes from the Old Testament. ☐

c) The parable of the Good Samaritan tells how a priest helped a Samaritan who had been beaten and robbed. ☐

d) Samaritans were unpopular in Jesus' time because they were mixed race. ☐

e) Martin Luther King made a famous speech where he said 'I have a dream'. ☐

f) Martin Luther King led the British Movement Against Apartheid. ☐

g) Trevor Huddleston was a black South African. ☐

h) Trevor Huddleston was a friend of Desmond Tutu. ☐

War and peace

8 Match the descriptions in the left-hand column of the table with the words below.

boycott   Thomas Aquinas   Martin Luther King
Quakers (Religious Society of Friends)   conscientious objectors

A Christian denomination that is traditionally pacifist	
He wrote about the conditions necessary for a Just War	
People whose consciences tell them not to fight	
A method of non-violent protest	
A famous Christian who was a pacifist	

9 Here are some of the conditions given for a Just War. What are the others?

The war must be declared by a proper authority

There must be a good reason for the war

- _____

- _____

The war must do more good than harm

- _____

The methods used must be fair

Historical figures

10 Fill in the following table.

Name	What they did
Thomas Aquinas	
Charles Darwin	
Martin Luther King	
Pope Paul VI	
Amos	
Jesus	

God and the idea of the Trinity

1 That God has three persons: Father, Son and Holy Spirit but that they are all part of the same one God.

2 In the Creeds of the Christian Church such as the Apostles' Creed and the Nicene Creed.

The Bible

1 The Old Testament contains the books of the Jewish scriptures, the Tenakh, while the New Testament is about the life and teachings of Jesus and the early church.

2 Christians believe that the Bible is the word of God. Some people think that every word of the Bible is true and cannot be changed. Others believe that it needs to be interpreted for modern times.

Jesus

1 He had a human mother, Mary, but his father was God.

2 That people should treat everyone as if they were their neighbour.

The Ten Commandments

1 So that they knew how God wanted them to live and so that he would be pleased with his people and take care of them.

2 Because it reminds people that every week they should have a day of rest when they can concentrate on God. It recalls the fact that, after the Creation of the world, God rested on the seventh day.

The Sermon on the Mount

1 Because it was the only prayer that they needed and that they should use it rather than praying in public so that other people could see how holy they were.

2 He said that divorce was wrong unless the woman was unfaithful.

The problem of evil

1 You need to show that you understand why it is a problem – if God is perfectly good and able to do anything at all, then why doesn't he do something to stop evil things like terrorist attacks, diseases and wars? You need to concentrate on Christian responses, rather than on your own answer to this problem. Christians might say that the evil in the world is the result of the Fall of Adam and Eve, and not God's responsibility at all. They might say that we need evil in the world in order to learn and to exercise freedom of choice. Or they might say that evil is a mystery that we will never understand until after death.

2 You should restrict your answer to different Biblical examples rather than giving your own view. You might write about the Fall of Adam and Eve, and how this was seen as the beginning of pain. You could include reference to the Devil, perhaps mentioning the book of Job or the story of Jesus' temptations in the wilderness. You might write about how Jesus showed concern for those who were suffering, and about how the Bible teaches that Jesus came into the world to share in human suffering. You could include ideas about heaven, and the teaching that suffering won't exist in heaven.

3 You might think about how someone would support the statement, and explain what belief in the Devil involves. On the other hand, people might disagree with it for all sorts of reasons: some might say that there is no such thing as the Devil; some might say that people are to blame for evil, not the Devil. Remember that not all Christians would agree with this statement, although some would.

The Church – history

1 He was Jew from Tarsus who was employed to hunt out and persecute the early followers of Jesus. In approximately 35 CE, he had a vision that Jesus called him. His name was changed to Paul and he began to preach the message of Christianity throughout the Mediterranean.

2 Because there were differences over Christian teachings, because people wanted to worship in different ways.

Christian denominations

1 Because some people believed that the Roman Catholic Church in the 16th century was corrupt. They no longer recognised the authority of the Pope and wanted to follow their own religious leaders.

2 King Henry VIII had an argument with the Pope because he wanted a divorce which the Roman Catholic church would not allow. Therefore, the King made himself head of the Church.

Ecumenism

1 Some believe that women should have an equal role with men in all aspects of their religion. Others think that men and women are different and that priests should be men because the first disciples were all men.

2 A place such as Taizé or Iona where Christians from different denominations meet and worship together.

The church - buildings and features

1 The altar.

2 The font is a receptacle for baptising babies. Some churches have a pool instead of a font.

3 The cross is one of the main Christian symbols, representing the crucifix on which Jesus died.

4 These are often seen as a sign of reaching up to God.

Pilgrimage

1 To strengthen their faith, in the hope of a cure for themselves or someone else, to visit relics of the saints, to visit places associated with Jesus.

2 Although some people like to visit certain places on a pilgrimage, others believe that a real pilgrimage is exploring your own soul and finding the right way to reach God, therefore, a pilgrimage is a journey that takes a person's whole life.

Prayer

1 Adoration, confession, corporate, intercessory, petitionary, private, public, set prayer, spontaneous prayer, thanksgiving.

2 Because it reminds them of the fact that Jesus was the Son of God but born from a human mother and shows them what a good and holy woman Mary was.

Baptism

1 Because Christians believe that Adam and Eve brought sin into the world when they disobeyed God and that everyone is born with this Original Sin.

2 Baptism takes place when someone is already an adult and people are baptised by total immersion.

The Eucharist

1 'This is my body, which is for you; do this in remembrance of me.' 'This cup is the new covenant in my blood; do this, whenever you drink it, in remembrance of me.'

2 Lord's Supper, Mass, Holy Communion, Breaking of Bread.

3 Because Christians are united together as they share the body and blood of Christ.

Confirmation

1 So that they can be prepared for the importance of the ceremony they are going through and so that they are sure that they know the teachings of Christianity.

2 Some denominations do not have confirmation because they practise adult baptism.

3 The candidates for confirmation are questioned by the Bishop to make sure that they accept Jesus and reject the devil. Then the Bishop blesses each person by putting his hand on their heads as a sign of the Holy Spirit.

Funerals

1 As a sign of respect and sadness.

2 It reminds people that the body is unimportant and it is the soul that lives on.

Life after death

1 It is not clear whether it is a physical or spiritual life but it teaches that people who follow Jesus' teachings will go to heaven.

2 Because they do not think that everyone is ready to go to heaven when they die but they have lived good lives as so are not sent to hell.

The Christian year

1 Although Christmas marks the incarnation, the birth of Jesus, it is at Easter that Christians remember his sacrifice on the cross.

2 It means that every year people have the opportunity to recall all the important events in the life of Jesus.

Advent and Christmas

1 The incarnation is the birth of Jesus, when God came to earth in human form.

2 Christians do not believe that Jesus was born on December 25th – they do not know when he was born. The date was fixed in 354CE by Pope Gregory so that people celebrated Christmas at a time when, in the past, they would have celebrated pagan festivals.

Lent, Holy Week and Easter

1 Because it was the time when Jesus was crucified and came back from the dead. It showed that Jesus was really the Son of God and had the power to overcome death.

2 To try to make themselves stronger and to resist temptation. Also to show that they are sorry for their sins and are preparing themselves to remember Jesus' suffering.

Ascension and Pentecost

1 When Jesus finally left his disciples and went up to heaven.

2 A Thursday.

3 A Sunday.

4 Whitsun means White Sunday because of the white clothes that many people used to wear for this festival.

5 Because it was the time when the disciples received the Holy Spirit and began to preach Jesus' message to other people.

6 Acts of the Apostles.

Caring for the poor

1 You might include something from the prophets (Amos), to show that poverty has always been a problem and that caring for the poor has always been a part of showing love for God. You could include some of Jesus' teaching, such as the 'Golden Rule' or some examples of parables.

2 People who agree might say that the Bible teaches that loving God always goes with loving other people, and that God says people who do nothing for the poor will be punished after death. So perhaps it is impossible to be a Christian if you do nothing to help the poor, because your faith can't mean very much if you don't put it into practice. People who disagree might say that not everyone can help the poor, but they might still be good Christians in other ways – perhaps if they are very old, or very poor themselves, or disabled or only young without their own money, they wouldn't be able to do much for the poor. But they could still be good Christians because of their beliefs. Don't forget to include your own opinion.

Christian aid agencies

1 You might choose CAFOD, Christian Aid or Tearfund, for example. You are asked to describe the work, so you could include emergency aid and long-term projects. You might think about health care, immunisation, education, clean water provision and disaster relief. You could also write about how the organisation raises funds, for example, you might refer to Christian Aid week or fasting for CAFOD.

2 You might include the idea of agape (Christian love) and the command to treat other people as you would like to be treated yourself, and to love your neighbour as you love yourself. You might write about the belief that all people are equally valuable to God, perhaps including a reference to Genesis. You could include parables, such as the Sheep and the Goats. You could refer to the teaching of the prophets about concern for the poor.

Money and wealth

1 You might include examples such as the Parable of the Rich Fool, or the Parable of the Talents, or the story of the widow who gave all she had. You might include some Old Testament teaching such as rules about dealing honestly with other people and looking after those in need.

2 You could include the way the money is earned; a Christian would believe that money must be earned honestly, in a job that doesn't exploit other people. You might think about how a Christian would spend the money; he or she might think it is important to take a responsible attitude towards other members of the family, and not spend all the money at the pub on the way home without thinking about what the children will eat. You could include the idea that Christians might put aside some of the money for charity, rather than spending it all on themselves, or they might help out another family member or a neighbour rather than keeping everything.

3 Perhaps some people would agree with the statement by saying that the important thing is to earn the money honestly, and then people should be able to enjoy the money. If they have worked hard and want to spend the money on going out or having a nice holiday, they deserve that. A different Christian point of view might be that people shouldn't give themselves expensive treats when there are other people in the world who are starving, and that some of the money should go to charity.

The sanctity of life

1 You need to be able to explain that Christians think that human life is special, different from other forms of life. You could use examples to illustrate your answer, such as showing that you know that in Genesis, God creates humanity as the most important part of creation, 'in his own image'. In the Psalms, God is said to know each individual from the moment of conception. You might want to write something about the implications of this idea, such as how belief in the sanctity of life might affect attitudes towards issues like abortion, euthanasia, embryo research or capital punishment.

2 In this answer, you need to show that you can apply the teaching about the sanctity of life to a particular issue – abortion. You could say that if Christians believe that life is sacred, they might be against abortion, because they might believe that God values every human life from the moment of conception and therefore this life should not be destroyed. You should show that you understand what is meant by 'sanctity of life', perhaps by using examples from the Bible.

3 This statement is suggesting that euthanasia should be allowed if life is sacred, because when people want

euthanasia, it is often because they are suffering severe pain, and perhaps this pain spoils something that is meant to be special. But most Christians would argue that the opposite is true – if life is holy, then it should be preserved even when people are suffering, because only God has the right to take away life.

Contraception (birth control)

1   You should make it clear that you understand what contraception is, but you shouldn't spend a large part of your answer describing different methods and their effectiveness. Instead, you should concentrate on Christian attitudes. Some Christians, particularly Roman Catholics, believe that artificial contraception is wrong because it can prevent a human life being born when God might have wanted that child to come into the world. Others believe that it is sensible and practical to limit the number of children that couples have.

2   Roman Catholics, in particular, are likely to agree with the statement, and argue against the use of artificial contraception. Other people might disagree and perhaps say that it can put a strain on a marriage if a couple have more children than they can easily afford to bring up.

Fertility treatment and embryo research

1   Some Christians believe that fertility treatment is always worthwhile, because it helps couples to bring new life into the world, and human life is always valuable. Others argue that there can be problems, for example, when 'spare' embryos have to be created in order to give the woman a reasonable chance of a successful pregnancy. Some people think that embryos shouldn't be treated as 'spare' but should be recognised as human life. Some Christians also feel that it is wrong to interfere with nature in this way, and that if a couple can't have children naturally, perhaps this means that God doesn't want them to become parents. You might also think about people who want fertility treatment when they are in homosexual relationships or are past the natural age of child-bearing, and consider what a Christian might say about those situations.

2   Christians might say that medicine is important and that Jesus was a healer, but that it isn't right just to ignore problems that arise from embryo research, such as deciding what to do with 'spare' embryos. You could consider another point of view, such as the view that if embryos are unwanted, there is no harm in experimenting on them; and you also need to decide what your own view is about this.

Abortion

1   The question asks for Christian teaching, so you can include the Bible as well as other teachings such as statements from Church leaders. Remember that the Bible doesn't say very much directly related to abortion, but it does have passages about the sanctity of life and about God knowing each person before they are born, so you might want to make reference to those. You could also refer to Biblical teaching about treating others as you would like to be treated yourself, and explain how this could be used to justify an abortion in some cases. You might be able to refer to the teaching of the Roman Catholic Church, and to other Christian denominations as well, showing that you realise that not all Christians have the same views on this issue.

2   Some think that abortion can be the kindest thing to do, if the mother is very young, or if there are signs to show that the baby isn't developing normally and could be severely handicapped. They might think that it would be cruel to make someone who was pregnant as a result of rape go through with the pregnancy, and they might think that the pregnancy doesn't count as a human life before the baby is born. Other Christians believe that abortion is wrong, because it involves taking away the life of an unborn child. They believe that human life begins at the moment of conception and that it is wrong to choose to destroy a life which belongs to God. You could refer to the teachings of different churches, and show that you know that Roman Catholic teaching is more firmly against abortion than the teachings of some of the other Christian churches.

3   Some people think that abortion is the same as murder because they think that life begins as soon as conception takes place. Roman Catholics tend to take this position. Other people think that the foetus isn't the same as a person, and therefore abortion isn't the same as murder because it doesn't take away someone who already exists. Remember to give your own view and to justify it with reasons.

Euthanasia

1   Some Christians believe that euthanasia can be the most loving answer, if someone is in terrible pain or has lost all their independence. They might say that we would help our pets to end their lives without pain, so we should show the same concern for other human beings too. Other Christians believe that only God has the right to take away life, and that sometimes God might use suffering in order to teach people and bring them closer to him. You might be able to use Biblical examples to support your answer, or refer to teachings from the churches.

2   You need to think here about how a Christian would

feel, if they had a husband or wife or parent or child who wanted euthanasia. What might they say, and why? Perhaps they would agree, thinking of Jesus' teaching that you should always treat others in the way you would like to be treated yourself. Or perhaps they would tell the relative that only God has the right to end a life, and that they will do all they can to ease the pain but that they can't help with euthanasia. Remember that not all Christians would respond in the same way to this issue.

3   This question is asking about how much quality of life matters when people are making decisions about life and death. Is a life full of pain still worth living? Some people would say that it is worthwhile to God, even if it is painful, and that every human being is made in the image of God, whatever their quality of life. Others might argue that if you can't enjoy life and are suffering, it is better if the life ends.

The hospice movement

1   Dame Cicely Saunders, in 1967.

2   Hospices are places where people who are terminally ill can spend the ends of their lives and receive medical treatment to make them more comfortable. They are also places where people who are normally cared for at home can go for a break, to give the carers a rest. Hospices provide counselling and support, to help patients and their families prepare for death. They often continue to support the family once the patient has died.

3   In this answer you are being asked to explain how and why – so you should think about how Christians might support a hospice – for example, through fund-raising, prayer, or voluntary work. You also need to think about why Christians might support it – you could include ideas such as that Christians believe in the value of all human life, and tend to be against euthanasia, so they want to help people to die with dignity and without pain at a time chosen by God.

War

1   For this answer you need to show that you realise that Biblical material can be used to support fighting in a war, but can also be used to defend a pacifist position. You might include references to the 'holy wars' of the Old Testament, and to times when God seemed to command people to go out and fight – you could also refer to ideas about peace and about loving enemies and working as peace-makers.

2   In this answer, you need to show that you understand the teaching of Thomas Aquinas about the different ways in which to judge whether a war is just, or fair. You should be able to explain as many of the different points as you can remember – for example, the ideas that the war must be started by a proper

authority. For high marks in questions like these, you need to have revised thoroughly and be able to put as much detail as you can into your answers.

3   In this answer you should consider arguments for and against pacifism. You need to be able to explain different points of view – for example, you might say that some Christians feel that it's important to defend the weak in times of war and to be loyal to their countries. Other Christians, such as the Quakers, feel that violence is never justified, even in war-time, and that it is better to risk being killed by the enemy than to act in a violent way. You might be able to give Biblical examples to justify these points of view.

Human rights

1   You might include Biblical teaching about Christian love, and always treating others in the way that you would like to be treated yourself. You could include the parable of the Sheep and the Goats, and say that Christians believe that God will judge them on the basis of the how they have cared for other people, including those in prison. You might write about teachings which show that God cares for and values each individual, and that everyone is united in Christ.

2   Remember that Amnesty International isn't a Christian organisation. But Christians might choose to support it, because they believe that everyone is valuable to God and made in the image of God. Christians might support it as a way of showing Christian love to prisoners of conscience and victims of torture. They might believe that it is their duty to fight against evil and injustice. They might want to treat political prisoners in the way that they would want to be treated if they were in that position.

Capital punishment

1   This question requires you to give specific examples of Christian teachings. You could refer to the 'eye for eye' passage, or give examples of times where God seemed to be punishing people with death. You could refer to the time when Jesus told people that the first one to begin stoning the woman caught in adultery should be the person who hadn't committed a sin, showing that no-one has the right to condemn others. You might want to quote a passage about forgiveness or about Christian love. Try to give several different examples, rather than explaining just one at length.

2   Some people might argue that capital punishment is the same as murder because both involve deliberately taking away a human life. They might say that the executioner becomes as bad as the criminal. Others could argue that capital punishment is done for good reasons, as a deterrent and to protect the rest of society, even to protect the criminal from many years

in jail, and so it isn't the same as murder. Remember to include Christian views – perhaps there would be Christians on each side of this debate.

Pacifism

1   You can use some of your information from your studies of the Just War in this answer. You need to show why some Christians believe that war is never justified, and how they believe that enemies should be treated with love and only peaceful means of defence should be used. You could use Biblical quotations here, and you might want to say something about the beliefs of the Quakers (Religious Society of Friends).

2   This question requires you to think about the practical applications of a pacifist outlook. Perhaps Christians would go on marches and other forms of demonstration, particularly those which protest against wars. They might join petitions or campaign groups to try and stop their countries from waging war. In peace-time, they might try to take non-aggressive approaches to situations at school or at work. They might take part in fund-raising for peace-promoting organisations, and they might pray for peace. If you have visited Coventry Cathedral during your GCSE course, you could include something about that. You might have studied people who have worked for peace in places like Northern Ireland.

Prejudice

1   There are several different examples you could use here, and you should try to mention a selection of ideas rather than just one. The parable of the Good Samaritan is an obvious choice – but you only need to explain the message of the parable, you don't need to write it all out in full. You might also include teaching about treating all people as valuable because they are made in the image of God, and you could refer to Old Testament teachings about the right ways to behave towards immigrants who move into your country. You could include ideas about Christian love (agape), and about treating others in the way that you would like to be treated yourself.

2   Christians might join organisations which campaign for racial equality. They could welcome ethnic minorities into their neighbourhoods, and support local events which celebrate different ethnic traditions. They could make sure that they bring up their children with non-racist attitudes, and they could try to make sure that their friends and colleagues know that they disapprove of racist jokes. They could volunteer to help with Victim Support and visit people who have been the victims of racial attacks. They could try and encourage their employers to implement equal opportunities policies when they are recruiting.

The struggle against racism

1   You should make sure that the person you choose to write about is a Christian, rather than an anti-racist activist with no particular religious affiliation. Martin Luther King or Trevor Huddleston would be good choices, although you may have studied someone else and want to write about that person instead. The question asked why, as well as how, they have worked against racism, so you need to include something about their Christian beliefs. You could say that their beliefs made them realise that everyone is made in the image of God, whatever their colour, and then go on to explain what they did.

2   There are several points to consider here. You might think about whether Christians always have a duty to do something about racism, or whether racism is something that can sometimes be ignored. You also need to think about what the statement means by 'fight'. It could mean opposition in all sorts of ways, such as peaceful protests, but it could also mean using violence. You might write about whether it can be right for Christians to fight racism with violence, or whether they should always choose peaceful protests, as Martin Luther King argued.

Family

1   You need to show that you understand that Christians believe that the family is important for a stable society, and that God planned that men and women should marry and have children. You might say that many Christians believe that having children is an important duty for Christians, as a way of continuing the human race and as a way of passing the Christian faith on from generation to generation. You could say that Christians believe that families are a good place to learn about love, loyalty and commitment.

2   When you are answering this question, you should consider different points of view. Some people might think that Christianity is the truth, and that parents have duty to tell the truth to their children and make them go to church. They might think that if parents left it to their children to choose, then the children would choose not to follow the Christian faith because they wouldn't realise that it was important. Other people might think that this can have the wrong effect, and that if you try and make children do something, then it could turn them against Christianity altogether.

3   In this answer, you might refer to an organisation such as the Mothers' Union. You could say that Christians might support it because they believe that the family is an important part of society. Christians

believe that a stable family can bring up the next generation to follow Christian principles, and that a family can provide hospitality and care for those in need. Because they believe that the family is important, they might support an organisation which cares for the families of prisoners, and which support single parents, and which encourages good parenting.

Gender

1   This question asks for an explanation of Christian teaching, so you could use references from the Bible or from any other Christian source. You might refer to Biblical teaching, such as the story of Adam and Eve, or the teaching in Galatians about everyone being equal in Christ. For high marks, you could show that you recognise that the Bible could be interpreted in different ways on this issue. You might also refer to Church teaching, and you could include discussion about the ordination of women.

2   In this answer, you should show that you understand why people might agree or disagree with this statement, and also give your own opinion. You might say that some people follow the teachings of the Bible literally, and believe that a woman's role is to obey her husband and support him in what he does – he should be the leader in the relationship. Other people might disagree and say that men and women are both made in the image of God and should have equal rights. It could be argued that this teaching is old-fashioned and not appropriate for today's society.

3   This question asks you to show understanding of why Christians might have different opinions about the ordination of women. Some Christians think that women should be able to be leaders in the church on the same basis as men, as long as they have the necessary skills – you might be able to give examples of churches that have always had women in the ministry, such as the Salvation Army or the URC. Other Christians, such as Roman Catholics, believe that only men should be priests, because Christ is represented when the bread and wine are blessed during the Eucharist, and this is only appropriate for men. You could mention that Jesus only had male apostles – but perhaps this was because of first-century society rather than because women should not have this role.

Marriage and divorce

1   This question asks you to evaluate whether marriage should be for life, or whether this is an unrealistic expectation. You might say that Christians believe that marriage should be a lifelong commitment, and that part of the marriage service involves promising to stay together until death. You could also say that

some Christian churches don't allow divorce, but expect people to stay married for life. Another point of view might be to say that the statement is true, and that although people might intend to stay together when they marry, there are lots of reasons why sometimes this is impossible.

2   Notice that the question asks about the importance of marriage, so you should write about why Christians think that marriage is an important part of life, rather than for example describing a wedding ceremony. You might include a reference to Genesis, where God makes Adam and Eve to be a couple; you might write about the importance of marriage in Christian teaching as the best context for bringing up children. You could include teachings about how wives should support their husbands. You might explain how marriage is seen as a symbol of the relationship between Christ and the church, and that in Roman Catholic teaching, marriage is a sacrament (a sign of God's grace).

3   In this answer you need to show that you realise that the Christian churches have different teachings about the ethics of divorce. You should show that you understand that Roman Catholics don't recognise divorce, because they consider that marriage is a sacrament which can't be undone. But most of the other Christian churches teach that divorce is acceptable when a marriage has broken down, even though it is a serious decision and the couple should make an effort to keep their marriage together rather than getting divorced at the first sign of trouble.

The environment

1   This question asks you to show understanding of how Christians might put their beliefs into practice. You need to show that you know what the beliefs are – here, you might explain Christian beliefs that the world is God's creation and that people exist to be 'stewards' or caretakers of the earth. You also need to give examples of practical ways in which Christians might demonstrate these beliefs – for example, Christians might use 'green' methods of transport, they might make an effort to use recycling facilities, and they might buy products which have been produced by environmentally friendly methods.

2   For this answer you should show knowledge of the reasons Christians might have for supporting an agency which works to protect the environment. You could mention specific organisations, such as Friends of the Earth or Greenpeace, but the main point of your answer should focus on giving Christian reasons for supporting it. You might say that Christians believe that people have a responsibility for the planet, as 'stewards of the earth'; you could say that Christian love for other people involves care for future generations.

3   Remember that you need to show understanding of different points of view. You could say that some people might agree, because if Christians don't care for the environment and dangers such as global warming are allowed to get worse, the future of humanity could be at risk. Other people might argue that caring for the environment is best cared for by politicians or conservationists, and that Christians should concern themselves with other things, such as prayer or caring for the poor.

Science and religion

1   In this answer, you are meant to show your skill in evaluation. You need to show why some people might think that the statement is true – they might think that scientific accounts of how things happened, such as the beginning of the world or the origins of species, disprove religious ideas. Other people might believe that the Bible is the exact word of God, and therefore that the Bible is always literally true, so that if science says something different, science must be wrong. Remember also to give your own view, and try to justify it with a reason.

2   You need to show that you understand that there are some Christians who take the Biblical stories literally, and others who believe that science and religion can be compatible. Some Christians might believe that the world was created exactly as described in Genesis, in six days. Others might think that the Genesis story is a myth, and that God did create the world but not necessarily in exactly that way – perhaps God created the Big Bang, for example, or perhaps God designed evolution.

Religion and media

1   In your answer, you might show that you recognise that the media are methods of communication. People don't object to the media themselves, but to some of the ideas and messages portrayed in the media. Christians might think that the media have advantages, because they can be used as a way of communicating Christian beliefs and ideas. They can be used to make people aware of issues such as famines, where they might be able to help. Christian services of worship can be broadcast through the media. On the other hand, the media might be seen to have disadvantages because it can encourage attitudes which go against Christian teaching. Some programmes seem to encourage violence, for example.

2   Some Christians might agree with the statement; they might think that there is too much violence on television, or they might think that television gives a bad impression of family life, or promotes the wrong sorts of values. They might believe that television advertising encourages people to be greedy and envious, and they might think that if families spend too much time watching television, they won't communicate with each other enough. But many Christians think that as long as people are sensible about what they watch, television can be a good way to relax and can also be used for getting the Christian message across, and for keeping people informed about what's happening in the world.

Key terms

> • Most of the key terms in Christianity are familiar in English, although some come from the Greek of New Testament times and others come from Hebrew.

A

Abortion the termination of a pregnancy before the foetus has reached full term

Advent the period beginning on the fourth Sunday before Christmas. A time of spiritual preparation for Christmas

Agape Christian love, love that does not depend on anything

Altar (Communion Table, Holy Table) table used for Eucharist, Mass, Lord's Supper. Some denominations refer to it as Holy Table or Communion Table

Anglican churches whose origins and traditions are linked to the Church of England

Apostle somene who was sent out by Jesus Christ to preach the Gospel

Ascension the event, forty days after the Resurrection, when Jesus ascended into heaven (see Luke 24 and Acts 1)

Ash Wednesday the first day of Lent. In some Churches, penitents receive the sign of the cross in ashes on their foreheads

B

Baptism rite of initiation involving immersion in, or sprinkling of, water

Big Bang scientific theory suggesting that the universe was formed from a massive explosion of gases

C

Christ (Messiah) the anointed one. 'Messiah' is used in the Jewish tradition to refer to the expected leader sent by God, who will bring salvation to God's people. Jesus' followers applied this title to him, and its Greek equivalent, Christ, is the source of the words Christian and Christianity

Church (i) the whole community of Christians; (ii) the building in which Christians worship; (iii) a particular denomination

Creed a summary statement of religious beliefs, often recited in worship, e.g. the Apostles' and Nicene Creeds

Crucifixion Roman method of executing criminals and traitors by fastening them to a cross until they died of asphyxiation; used in the case of Jesus Christ and many who opposed the Romans

E

Easter central Christian festival which celebrates the resurrection of Jesus Christ from the dead

Embryo research medical research using human embryos

Eucharist a service celebrating the sacrificial death and resurrection of Jesus Christ, using elements of bread and wine (see Holy Communion). Eucharist means 'thanksgiving'

Euthanasia 'good death'; bringing about the end of a person's life to give them a more dignified death

F

Fertility treatment medical treatment designed to help people to conceive a child

Font receptacle to hold water used in baptism

G

Good Friday the Friday in Holy Week. Commemorates the day Jesus died on the cross

Gospel (Evangel) (i) good news (of salvation in Jesus Christ); (ii) an account of Jesus' life and work

H

Heaven the place, or state, in which souls will be united with God after death

Hell the place, or state, in which souls will be separated from God after death

Holy Communion central service for most churches (see Eucharist, Mass). Recalls the last meal of Jesus and celebrates his sacrificial and saving death

Holy Spirit the third person of the Holy Trinity. Works as God's power in the world, and lives in Christians to help them to follow Christ

Holy Week the week before Easter, when Christians remember the last week of Jesus' life on Earth

Hospice a hospital specialising in the care of the dying

I

Iconostasis A screen, covered with icons, used in Eastern Orthodox churches to separate the sanctuary from the nave

J

Jesus Christ the central figure of Christian history and devotion. The second person of the Trinity

Just War doctrine teaching about the conditions necessary for a war to be fair and right

L

Lectern a stand supporting the Bible, often in the shape of an eagle

Lent season of repentance. The forty days leading up to Easter

M

Mass term for the Eucharist, used by the Roman Catholic and other churches

Maundy Thursday the Thursday in Holy Week which commemorates the Last Supper

N

New Testament collection of 27 books forming the second section of the Canon of Christian Scriptures

Non-conformist Protestant Christian bodies which separated from the established Church of England in the 17th century

O

Old Testament the part of the Canon of Christian Scriptures which the Church shares with Judaism, containing 39 books covering the Hebrew Canon. Some churches also include some books of the Apocrypha

124

Ordination the 'laying on of hands' on priests and deacons by a bishop

Orthodox the Eastern Orthodox Church consisting of national Churches (mainly Greek or Slav), including the ancient Eastern Patriarchates

Pacifism the belief that violence is never right

Palm Sunday the Sunday before Easter, commemorating the entry of Jesus into Jerusalem when crowds waved palm branches

Passion the sufferings of Jesus Christ, especially in the time leading up to his crucifixion

Pentecost (Whitsun) the Greek name for the Jewish Festival of Weeks, or Shavuot, which comes seven weeks ('fifty days') after Passover. On the day of this feast, the followers of Jesus received the gift of the Holy Spirit

Pope the Bishop of Rome, head of the Roman Catholic Church

Prejudice making a judgement without any evidence

Protestant that part of the Church which became distinct from the Roman Catholic and Orthodox Churches when their members professed (or 'protested') the centrality of the Bible and other beliefs

Pulpit a raised platform from which sermons are preached

Purgatory in some traditions, a condition or state in which good souls receive spiritual cleansing after death, in preparation for heaven

Q

Quakers (Religious Society of Friends) a Christian church committed to pacifism

R

Racism the belief that some races are superior to and more valuable than others

Resurrection (i) the rising from the dead of Jesus Christ on the third day after the crucifixion; (ii) the rising from the dead of believers at the Last Day; (iii) the new, or risen, life of Christians

Roman Catholic the part of the Church owing loyalty to the Bishop of Rome, as distinct from Orthodox and Protestant Churches

S

Sacrament an outward sign of an inward blessing, as in baptism or the Eucharist

Sanctity of life the belief that life is sacred

Selling of indulgences the Church practice of selling 'certificates' to Christians that exempted the believer from having to do 'good works' as part of their penance for sin

Sin disobedience against the will of God; falling away from the perfection of God

T

Trinity three persons in one God; belief that God's nature has three parts – Father, Son and Holy Spirit

U

Unction (Sacrament of the Sick) the anointing with oil of a sick or dying person

Last-minute learner

God and the idea of the Trinity

- Christians believe that there is only one God. They are monotheists.
- Christians also believe that God can be understood in three different ways, as the three 'persons' of the Trinity: God the Father, God the Son, and God the Holy Spirit.

The Bible

- The Bible is the most important and holy book in Christianity.
- Christians believe that the Bible is the 'Word of God', and a way in which God communicates to humanity.
- Christians try to understand the messages of the Bible, and to put them into practice in their daily lives.

Jesus

- Christians believe that Jesus Christ was the Son of God.
- Jesus gathered around him a group of men who are known as the Twelve Disciples. They were all working men from Galilee.
- Jesus preached in the open and attracted enormous crowds wherever he went. He performed many other miracles during his ministry in Galilee, in particular healing sick people, making the lame walk and the blind see.
- Most of his teaching was in parables. These were stories which his listeners could easily understand but which had a very important message.
- Jesus angered the Jewish authorities particularly by his teaching and the Jewish priests were alarmed by the claim that Jesus was the Messiah.

The Ten Commandments

- The Ten Commandments are ten rules which Jews and Christians believe were made by God, and given to Moses to pass on to everyone else. They are part of the 'covenant', or agreement, made between God and humanity.

1. You shall have no other gods
2. You shall not worship idols
3. You shall not misuse the name of God
4. Remember the Sabbath day and keep it holy
5. Honour your father and mother
6. You shall not murder
7. You shall not commit adultery
8. You shall not steal
9. You shall not give false testimony against your neighbour
10. You shall not covet (be envious of) your neighbour's possessions

The Sermon on the Mount

- During his ministry, Jesus spent much of his time in and around Galilee, where he preached and performed miracles.
- Jesus often taught in parables about the Kingdom of God and about forgiveness. He delivered a sermon usually called the Sermon on the Mount when he was near to the Sea of Galilee (Matthew 5-7).
- During this sermon he taught people the Beatitudes and the Lord's Prayer.

Evil and suffering

- The problem of evil asks why there is evil and suffering in the world, if there is supposed to be an all-loving, all-powerful God.
- Some Christians say that evil was brought into the world by human sin, when Adam and Eve first disobeyed God.
- Others say that God planned challenges and difficulties for people so that they would face real choices and become mature.
- The book of Job teaches that people should not expect to understand what God chooses to do. They should accept suffering without complaint.

The Church – history

- Jesus of Nazareth – Jesus Christ was probably born around the year 3 BCE in Bethlehem in the Roman province of Judaea in what is now Israel.
- He was crucified around 30 CE by the Romans.
- After his death and resurrection he ascended to heaven and his disciples received the Holy Spirit. They started to preach Jesus' teachings.

- A Jew, Saul of Tarsus, was employed to hunt out and persecute these early followers of Jesus. One day, probably in 35 CE he had a vision that Jesus called him. His name was changed to Paul and he began to preach the message of Christianity throughout the Mediterranean.
- In 392 CE the Roman Emperor Theodosius I made Christianity the official religion of the Roman Empire.
- In 597 CE Augustine came to England and brought Christianity to the country.

- In 1054 CE there was a split between the churches in Rome and Byzantium over differences in teaching. These two groups became the Roman Catholic Church based in Rome with the Pope as its head and the Orthodox Church based in Byzantium under the Patriarch of Constantinople.
- In 1534 Henry VIII made himself head of the church. This broke the ties with the Roman Catholic Church and established the Church of England.

Christian denominations

- There are several thousand different denominations in Christianity.
- All these people are Christians who believe in the Trinity and that Jesus was the Son of God.
- These are three of the main groups within the Christian Church:
  - **Orthodox Church**
  - **Roman Catholic Church**
  - **Protestant Churches**

Ecumenism

Ecumenism is the name given to the belief that all churches should try to become more united. It is a movement which encourages Christians to worship together and forget their differences.

The church – buildings and features

- There are many different types of buildings in which Christians worship.
- Some of these are called churches or chapels.
- Some buildings are very large and elaborate whilst others may be small and plain.
- The type of building often reflects the style of worship which takes place in them.
- Main features: **altar, pulpit, font**

Pilgrimage

- For Christians a pilgrimage is a religious journey.
- Usually people travel to places that have a special holy significance for them.
- Sometimes people say that a pilgrimage is a journey within. Christians can see their lives as being a pilgrimage towards God.
- Places of pilgrimage include:
  Holy Land, Lourdes, Walsingham, Rome

Prayer

Prayer is a very important aspect of life and worship for all Christians.

- Petitionary prayer is when people ask God for something, for themselves or for other people.
- Intercessory prayer is when people ask God to intervene in the world at a time of crisis or when people are starving or suffering because of a disaster.
- Many prayers are said to thank God for creation and for life and existence in general.
- Other prayers are to ask God's help in leading a better life.
- Sometimes people use formal set prayers such as those found in the prayer books of the various churches.
- Many Christians pray spontaneously, taking an opportunity to speak to God.

Sacraments

Baptism

- Christians believe that, because of the disobedience of Adam and Eve in the garden of Eden, all people are born with original sin.
- This sin needs to be removed before people can truly live their lives as Christians.
- In most churches this cleansing of sin takes place when a young baby is baptised.

Confirmation

- Confirmation is one of the sacraments of the Christian Church.
- The Roman Catholic Church has seven sacraments: baptism, confirmation, reconciliation, eucharist, ordination, marriage, anointing of the sick.
- A sacrament is said to be an outward visible sign of an inward spiritual grace.
- Confirmation is a celebration of when people decide for themselves to follow the Christian faith.

Funerals

- Christians believe that death is not the end of a person, although it is the end of their life on earth.
- Christian funerals reflect this belief. Although people are sad because a friend or relative or colleague has died, they are also encouraged to think about the promise of resurrection and eternal life made by Jesus. They are encouraged to ask for God's comfort, and to thank God for the good qualities the person had, rather than concentrating only on sadness.

Life after death

- Christians believe that when they die they will have the chance of eternal life.
- Christians believe that they may go to heaven, hell or purgatory, depending on how well they have lived one earth.

Advent and Christmas
- Advent is the four week period which leads up to Christmas.
- Christmas is one of the most important days in the Christian calendar.

Lent, Holy Week and Easter
- Lent is the six weeks of preparation which leads up to Easter, it also recalls the time that Jesus spent in the desert when he was tempted by the Devil.
- Easter is the most important festival in the whole of the Christian year, because is celebrates the resurrection of Jesus from the dead on Easter Sunday.
- Ascension and Pentecost.

Ascension Day and **Pentecost** are two important events in the church calendar which take place after Easter.

Medical ethics
- Christians believe that human life is sacred because people are made 'in the image of God'.
- Most Christians believe that abortion and euthanasia are wrong, because they take away human life. Some Christians think that they are acceptable in some circumstances, but the Roman Catholic church teaches that it is never acceptable to plan deliberately to end a human life.
- Most Christians think that it is sensible and responsible for people to use contraception, but the Roman Catholic church teaches that artificial methods of contraception go against 'natural law'.
- Many Christians are in favour of fertility treatment as long as it does not involve destroying human embryos.

Poverty and wealth
- Christianity teaches that all Christians have a responsibility to care for the poor.
- It teaches that it is wrong to be rich when other people are hungry.
- The parable of the Sheep and the Goats, and the parable of the rich man and Lazarus, are examples of teachings Christians might use in a discussion about poverty.
- CAFOD, Christian Aid and Tearfund are all examples of Christian aid agencies involved in helping the poor. They try to help developing countries to be less dependent on overseas aid, and they give money to long-term projects as well as emergency relief.

War, peace and justice

War and peace
- Thomas Aquinas set out the conditions for a Just War in the Middle Ages. Many Christians believe that this is the right approach to issues of war.
- Some Christians are pacifists. They believe that it is never right to use aggression and violence towards enemies. The Quakers (Religious Society of Friends) are traditionally pacifist.
- Conscientious objectors are people who believe it is wrong to fight in wars.
- Christians disagree about whether war can be right, and Biblical support can be found for a variety of opinions.

Prejudice
- The Bible teaches that all people are made in the image of God and all have value.
- It teaches that Christians should treat other people as they would like to be treated themselves, whatever their race.
- The parable of the Good Samaritan is a good example of Christian teaching that could be used in a discussion about race.
- Martin Luther King and Trevor Huddleston are examples of Christians who have worked against racism.
- Some Christians believe that men and women should have equal rights, responsibilities and opportunities. Others believe that men should have a leadership role and women should have a caring role. Support for both points of view can be found in the Bible.

The family
- Christians believe that people have the choice whether to marry or stay single. Jesus never married.
- Christians believe that marriage should be for life. Some Christian churches allow the remarriage of divorced people. The Roman Catholic church does not recognise divorce.
- Relate is an example of an organisation which helps people in relationships, and Christians might support it.
- The family is believed to have an important role to play in Christian life, as a source of love, hospitality, education and stability.
- The Mothers'Union is an example of a Christian organisation which supports family life.

Marriage
- The Bible teaches that God made the two different sexes so that they could join together in marriage as a life-long partnership.
- Christians believe that when a man and a woman are joined together in marriage, this is a symbol of the love Christ has for the church.

Global ethics

Science and religion

- Some Christians believe that scientific theories such as the Big Bang and Darwin's theory of natural selection are wrong, because they contradict the Bible.
- Other Christians believe that the Bible sometimes uses myth and poetry to explain things. They think that science and religion could both be right about the origins of the world, but in different ways.

The environment

- Christians believe that the world is God's creation.
- They believe that they have a responsibility to look after the planet, because God told people to be 'stewards' of the earth. They believe that future generations should be shown love and concern.

Religion and media

- Christians do not normally object to portrayals of Jesus in art or films or television.
- Some Christians believe that the media undermines Christian values when it shows too much violence, sex or marriage problems.